Building
Neighborhood
Confidence

Building Neighborhood Confidence

A Humanistic Strategy for Urban Housing

Rolf Goetze

Ballinger Publishing Company • Cambridge, Massachusetts
A Subsidiary of J.B. Lippincott Company

International Standard Book Number: 0-88410-442-7

Library of Congress Catalog Card Number: 76-7469

Printed in the United States of America

Library of Congress Cataloging in Publication Data

Goetze, Rolf.
    Building neighborhood confidence; a humanistic strategy for urban housing.

    Includes bibliographical references.
    1. Housing policy—Massachusetts—Boston metropolitan area. I. Title.
HD7304.B7G63   301.5'4   76-7469
ISBN 0-88410-442-7

Contents

List of Figures

List of Tables

Preface

In the belief that housing production could cure problems of housing blight, Boston has achieved an impressive amount of publicly assisted development in the last decade. But the familiar adage "is the glass half full or half empty" applies to the results. Many housing professionals are impressed by how far Boston has come in the last decade, while others show increasing concern about how far Boston has to go in coming years to remove housing blight.

This book is the outgrowth of efforts to delve into this situation and size up and define the tasks to be done in improving housing. This has involved many and taken over four years; and in the process many familiar assumptions crumbled and accepted approaches were overturned. Time and changing awareness have done their part. When this effort began great expectations still rested on the 1968 Housing Act and the production goals it set. But now, several years after the Nixon administration imposed a moratorium on production, many of the assisted developments are sliding towards foreclosure and it is questioned whether some can even last the forty year life of their mortgage. At the same time the national focus has shifted from new production to preserving the existing stock and understanding neighborhood dynamics.

Boston has averaged 2,000 dwelling units annually in production since 1960. Until 1967 the completed units included only a few produced under subsidy. However, by 1973 the situation reversed and most additions to the stock (still averaging around 2,000 units a year) were produced under mortgage subsidy and other special breaks like tax concessions. Whereas in 1965 less than $10,000 was required by a private contractor to produce a dwelling unit in Boston, over three times that amount is required only a decade later. The administrative costs associated with production have escalated so sharply that many accept that housing production and rehabilitation are no longer economically feasible without special subsidies. It seems contradictory that Boston also has a tight housing market, some housing abandonment, and rent control.

This book builds upon housing research and studies that I directed in the past several years at the Boston Redevelopment Authority (BRA). In 1972 the BRA and the Boston Urban Observatory (BUO), under National League of Cities funding, committed themselves to examine housing policy options towards two goals: alleviating housing substandardness and reducing the imbalances between the central city and the surrounding suburbs. The results of this undertaking include the inputs of many. This effort owes thanks to Robert T. Kenney, director of the BRA, William Grigsby of the University of Pennsylvania, and Joseph Slavet, director of the BUO at the University of Massachusetts in Boston, who initiated and encouraged the study. The BUO board members and especially Alex Ganz, who is director of the BRA Research Department as well, deserve shares in the credit. Without the BRA Research Department staff much less data analysis would have been possible. Kent Colton, who originally co-directed the study with me, Francine Price, Lowell Richards, Robert Earsey, Edward Blaine and Elizabeth Whitelaw Comer, all deserve thanks along with other BRA staff. John Weis and the BRA district planners under his direction helped shape the ideas presented in this book, and the Community Improvement Program (now the Housing Improvement Program) staff all furnished valuable inputs. And there have been countless community meetings and workshops with lenders, as well as sessions with the Mayor's staff and the new Office of Community Development which are reflected in this work.

Louise Elving and Tee Taggart of the BUO helped develop early drafts of the ideas presented here. For the patience in typing countless drafts of our housing studies while I was discovering what I was trying to say, Dorothy Anderson and Catherine Carroll must be especially singled out. The sources of inspiration cannot always be traced, so I apologize to any and all I may have inadvertently left out.

This book attempts a fresh approach to understanding housing dynamics and neighborhood revitalization. I accept the blame in advance for any errors, omissions, or oversimplifications I may have incurred in my eagerness to take the reader through these new concepts.

Rolf Goetze
Boston, Massachusetts
March 28th, 1976

Chapter 1

Introduction

In the wake of ambitious urban programs and turmoil of the 1960s, a new style of planning is emerging that is tempered by the harsher economic realities of today, and that demonstrates a humanistic approach that promises to radically modify the practices of the past. This "new planning" concentrates on people, perceptions, and ethnic considerations, and is based on understanding the dynamics of residential migration and the forces unleashed in neighborhood pluralism. This new approach is effectively coming to supplant the earlier planning focus on hard numbers—housing stock, condition, needs for fix-up and replacement. In the last decade planners increasingly vied for federal assistance, outdoing each other in calling attention to their urban problems until nearly everyone accepted the rhetoric that without federal dollars the end of our urban areas is in sight. In no small measure the supposed flight of the middle class and the retreat of urban lenders are a self-fulfilling consequence of the actions of those who were trying as best they knew to attract federal assistance. But now the time is at hand for a new approach that emphasizes the building of neighborhood confidence instead of units—and also explains the unexpected side effects of recent efforts: such as why urban renewal sometimes displaces instead of eradicates blight; why some HUD-subsidized developments with forty year mortgages become foreclosed within a decade; how increasing tenant-landlord polarization erodes sound housing; and why there are increasing charges of "red-lining" against lenders.

In Boston this new planning has been developing for several years, and planners in Boston increasingly find that colleagues facing similar challenges in other cities are probing similar new approaches. This book attempts to articulate elements of this new humanistic planning and to spell out the emerging insights to create discussion and hasten the day when this approach to planning gains more widespread acceptance.

WHY FOCUS ON BOSTON?

Boston offers a valuable case study for a wide audience, ranging from policymakers to students of urban dynamics and processes. Not only does Boston as a city continue to exert a strong attraction, but it is well explored by academic research, and an unusually strong data base has recently been developed. The Boston microcosm mirrors most of the national symptoms and efforts to deal with the "urban problem". Residential abandonment, disinvestment, as well as student neighborhood take-over, and aggressive implementation of federal programs of the 1960s have all occurred within a housing fabric that contains minority ghettoes and ethnic enclaves as well as sections that continue to hold the affluent and attract new luxury development. While conventional housing theory simply suggests that neighborhoods generally "filter" downward in quality, requiring renewal at the end, Boston has in fact been experiencing neighborhood recycling for decades, long before the special federal programs entered the scene. Now, as federally subsidized production again shrinks from the stage, understanding the basic forces that stabilize neighborhoods from decline and promote revitalization is reemerging as critical. Examined in light of the "new planning," the successes and failures of recent, federally-spurred housing strategies become more understandable, giving us valuable insights into the dynamics functioning both within and outside the influence of the recent federal interventions.

The current questions of housing policy move beyond concerns over national and local progress in meeting urban needs for standard shelter in a "livable" neighborhood within ability to pay. They focus rather on newer issues: freer housing choice; greater income and racial mix; flexible, market-oriented, region-wide, cost-effective housing policies; consumer-oriented housing subsidies; internal-incentive housing delivery systems.

Four decades of accumulated experience with a wide variety of national housing policies and local program responses to such policies have shown the limitations of symptom-oriented solutions. There is general agreement that housing production programs have left in their wake a plethora of unresolved related problems involving income, race, jobs, neighborhood, and the future of the central city. Four decades of past experience with housing programs have sharpened thinking about what housing policies *cannot* do for the poor and near-poor if they are less than clear in charting new directions for housing policy. New and rehabilitated housing, for example, can hardly rescue families from poverty since improved shelter does nothing about the basic needs of the poor for income, employment training, and educational opportunities. The evidence is also strong that families with housing needs place greater weight on neighborhood quality and services than on better shelter per se and that the purported beneficiaries of production-oriented housing subsidies are not noticeably aware of the dimension and value of such indirect housing assistance.[1]

In Boston, municipal attention is increasingly being given to sorting out the theoretical framework, data requirements, political ramifications, and value dimensions of housing policies. A number of line agencies are joined in this, including the Mayor's Office, the Boston Redevelopment Authority, which provides the city's basic research and planning capability, and the newly created Office of of Community Development.[2]

The objective of this book is to assist public officials and key persons concerned with housing policy in the comprehensive development of housing policies and strategies and to accomplish several related goals: (1) to improve the understanding of housing issues and alternative approaches for coping with them; (2) to link housing issues and proposed solutions with broader policies of community

1. See William G. Grigsby et al., *Housing and Poverty* (Institute for Environmental Studies, University of Pennsylvania, and Urban Studies Institute, Morgan State University April 1971), one of the earliest studies to point out the relative importance which inner-city residents gave to the neighborhood environment, particularly the nonphysical aspects thereof. Also see William Lilley III, "Toward A Rational Housing Policy," presented to Policy Committee Seminar on Community Development, 1973 Congress of Cities, San Juan, Puerto Rico, December 3, 1973.

2. Part of this growing in-house effort has been aided by National League of Cities funded collaboration between the Boston Redevelopment Authority and the Boston Urban Observatory in critical housing areas, resulting in three joint research reports of general interest conceptualized by the author: *Subsidized Multi-Family Rental Housing in the Boston Metropolitan Area: Analysis and Prognosis* (October 1973); *Working Class Housing—A Study of Triple Deckers in Boston* (May 1975); and *Housing Policy Considerations for a Central City in a Metropolitan Context; Boston, Mass.* (August 1975).

development; (3) to clarify how the private housing market really operates; and (4) to identify impediments to the implementation of housing policies and programs.

KEY ISSUES: HOUSING QUALITY AND HOUSING CHOICE

The following housing issues have been identified as of paramount interest to political leaders of central cities and their constituencies: (1) the quality of housing for present residents, and (2) the mix and choice of housing for varying income groups within and between the central city and other communities of the metropolitan area.

Quality. For Boston the quality of housing for all residents of the city has become an issue of prime concern. Since 1964, over one-twelfth of the city's housing stock has been renewed. A decade of highly visible, large-scale construction, mainly publicly-subsidized and carried out for the most part within the framework of urban renewal, has replaced a considerable amount of substandard, over-crowded housing with over 20,000 new and rehabilitated dwellings for all income groups and has discernably improved the general level of housing quality in several areas of the city. Over the three decades prior to 1960, the city had added almost 14,000 units of conventional public housing to its stock under a variety of federal and state subsidy programs. Moreover, the Boston Housing Authority, leasing agent for private housing under a separate subsidy program authorized by the Congress in 1965, had some 2,700 leased units under its jurisdiction by the end of 1973. In addition, federal and state rent supplement programs accounted for some 2,500 units and the Massachusetts Housing Finance Agency had authorized over 2,100 housing units serving families of mixed income in Boston. Altogether one in seven households in Boston lives in publicly-assisted housing.

Housing quality has become a major issue partly because of mounting resident complaints about conditions in federally-subsidized new and rehabilitated housing and their surrounding neighborhoods,[3] and even more because of the continuing deterioration of a large segment of the city's private housing and changes in the quality of neighborhoods located outside of designated urban renewal areas, neighborhoods largely untouched by federal policies and subsidies.

3. See report of Boston Redevelopment Authority and Boston Urban Observatory, *Subsidized Multi-Family Rental Housing in the Boston Metropolitan Area: Analysis and Prognosis* (October 1973).

Factors significantly affecting the quality of residential neighborhoods include housing abandonment, neighborhood segregation by income and race, the "red-lining" of selected neighborhoods by financial institutions and the exacerbation of landlord-tenant relations in multifamily rental housing.

The problem of inadequate housing quality encompasses neighborhoods containing both low- and moderate-income households, but is most critical in neighborhoods where low-income residents, particularly black and Spanish-speaking, predominate. Since the central city will for a long time in the future continue to perform its historical role as a primary houser of the poor and near-poor, particularly by serving as a waystation for many of the newest immigrants to the metropolitan area, it cannot avoid responsibility for facilitating access of this population to quality housing.

Choice. Related to the issue of housing quality, however, is the collateral question of how responsibility within the metropolitan area for housing the poor and near-poor should be shared among the various political jurisdictions. Should the central city and a few contiguous working class suburbs, for example, continue to be the primary places of settlement for population groups which depend on publicly-subsidized income maintenance and related social services? Or as Anthony Downs, Paul Davidoff, and most recently the city of Hartford have challenged, should the central city and its suburbs attempt to achieve a better socioeconomic balance and a job/housing balance during the next two decades?

The goal of better "balance" is being identified increasingly as a primary objective of housing and related public policies, particularly in land use control. In New Jersey, for instance, a balanced community has recently been accepted by the courts as a standard of the constitutionality of zoning ordinances.[4] A major difficulty with the concept of balanced community, however, is that it can mean different things in different times and places. It may be defined to include economic balance, racial balance, fiscal balance, ecological balance, regional balance, spatial balance, and temporal balance. A focus of this report is on issues of imbalance as they relate to income and race, since these are considered to be crucial aspects of Boston's current housing problem.

4. *Oakwood at Madison, Inc.* v. *Township of Madison,* 117 N.J. Super. 11 (1971). The New Jersey Superior Court held the entire zoning ordinance of Madison Township invalid because "it failed to promote reasonably a balanced community in accordance with the general welfare." See Jerome G. Rose, "The Courts and the Balanced Community: Recent Trends in New Jersey Zoning Law," *Journal of the American Institute of Planners* 39 (1973): 265.

Adverse Development Climate

Housing policy formulation must give appropriate weight to a public mood which no longer acquiesces to proposals for more physical development and particularly more housing. The prevailing attitude seems to be one of growing skepticism about development proposals, an attitude which has its origins in discontent and concern over the unpredictable consequences of new residential construction on the environment and on local tax rates. These have now been compounded by dwindling federal and state resource commitments, as well as the growing unwillingness of the financial market to participate in housing. Discontent and concern about change are entwined with a growing public mood for putting curbs on physical growth and for conserving existing neighborhood assets and values.

This prevailing negative mood against development and housing has been reinforced by shifts during the past few years in economic and housing policies, both nationally and locally. The trends are clear that new housing development in Boston has slowed. Over the past decade, the volume of Boston's privately-financed housing construction has declined steadily, while an increasing proportion of its new housing starts have been constructed with interest-reduction subsidies and rent supplements provided by the federal and state governments.[5] With the phasing-out of past federal mortgage support and with the general erosion of credit for construction and mortgage financing in financial markets, both private and subsidized, urban residential development is currently in serious decline. Sharply rising development costs, exacerbated by climbing interest rates and periodic capital shortages for construction and permanent financing, can be expected to deter construction of even middle-income housing throughout the nation, enhancing the value of the existing stock.

The rising mood against development is well illustrated by the organized efforts during the middle sixties and early seventies in many Boston neighborhoods against highway construction and urban renewal, particularly against high-rise residential construction and renewal activities ultimately benefiting upper-income groups as in the close-in South End and Fenway areas.

The trend in community development during recent years has

---

5. During the period 1967–73, some 15,800 housing units were completed in Boston, of which almost 59 percent were publicly subsidized. By contrast, during the prior seven-year period, only 14 percent of over 12,200 completed housing units were constructed with government assistance. With the increased dependence on federal subsidies, the recent curtailment of HUD production subsidies has sharply curtailed development. The effect on Boston has been a reduction of over 6,000 subsidized housing unit commitments during the 1971–73 period, as compared with the 1968–70 period; as a result, development is now down to a trickle.

been toward giving residents and neighborhood organizations greater participation in community development and housing activities affecting their areas. The federal government has encouraged this movement, for example, by requiring elected project advisory committees in urban renewal areas and calling for extensive citizen participation in formulating local plans under the Department of Housing and Urban Development's recent community development block grant program. The result of this new reality of officially recognized citizen participation is that development proposals almost anywhere in the city, even those designed to provide shelter for the elderly, must go through a much longer and more tortuous process of local review than formerly.[6] If a goal of expanded citizen participation in the development process was to increase the scope of resident support for housing or renewal proposals, this was achieved in some cases, although not through unanimous community consent. In other cases, however, organized citizen involvement has brought an unanticipated opposite result, increasing the number of persons intent on barring or drastically changing the nature and neighborhood impact of development proposals.[7]

Among the specific city policies which may be contributing to the adverse climate for housing development in Boston are rent control and property tax assessment and collection practices. Uncertainties about the tax consequences of recent court-ordered property revaluation and about the investment impacts of rent control tend to exacerbate the developers' perception of financial risk and to curb investment initiatives.[8]

6. See housing case studies in Morton Rubin, *Organized Citizen Participation*, prepared for Boston Urban Observatory, Part III (October 1971): 114–159.

7. This is illustrated by recent efforts to develop the Cabot estate in Boston. A developer had purchased the site in 1969 for the purpose of constructing two high-rise apartment towers containing 2,000 dwelling units. Community organizations strenuously opposed such high-density development and were particularly opposed to companion plans for intensive development of the park area contiguous to the residential site. Over a three-year period these organized efforts succeeded in thwarting the developer's application to the Zoning Board of Appeals for zoning variances. During this interval negotiations were conducted among representatives of the developer, community organizations and several city agencies, including the Boston Redevelopment Authority, the Mayor's Office, and the Office of Public Service. By the fall of 1973, these negotiations resulted in a drastic scaling-down of the proposed development to 165 clustered condominium units.

The point of the above example is that the "rules of the game" for getting development proposals approved had changed considerably since the sixties when the standard format for gaining city approval was an exciting proposal designed by a reputable architect.

8. Although local rent control legislation exempts structures constructed after January 1, 1969, luxury housing and substantially rehabilitated properties, and experimentation with vacancy decontrol has begun, there is the continuing fear that the legislature or city council may move to bring more recent residen-

Finally, recently enacted national and state environment impact statutes at least complicate if not discourage proposals for new housing development.[9] These laws require that the implementation of any new development proposal which is dependent upon public funds or upon public agency permits or certifications incorporate within its documentary justifications detailed environmental impact statements. As required by the federal government, these include five major components:

1. The environmental impact of the proposed action.
2. Any adverse environment effects which cannot be avoided should the proposal be implemented.
3. Alternatives to the proposed action.
4. The relationship between short-term uses of man's environment and the maintenance and enhancement of long-term productivity.
5. Any irreversible and irretrievable commitments of resources which would be involved in the proposed action should it be implemented.[10]

It should be noted that the scope of impact under federal law includes "man-made" as well as natural environment.

While the new environmental control laws are not inherently biased against development, their interpretation as to allegedly harmful environmental impacts can be and has been used to block publicly-assisted housing, high-rise residential construction and urban redevelopment. Not only can environmental control laws be used by affluent suburban communities to deter low and middle income housing developments with densities higher than surrounding residential areas, but environmental impact issues can pit relatively affluent conservation-oriented groups with secure assets and incomes

tial developments under rent control, thereby jeopardizing anticipated investment returns. As for assessment practices, although property tax policies in Boston for some new residential construction provide legitimate tax arrangements resulting in payments far below levels based on fair market value, there is growing apprehension about the impact of court-ordered equalization of property tax assessments to eliminate the current pattern of inequities between and within categories of real estate. The conclusion of a recent study of the impact of a 100 percent revaluation is that total assessed valuations would increase sharply in all residential categories. See Daniel M. Holland and Oliver Oldman, *Estimating the Impact of 100% Property Tax Assessments of Boston Real Estate*, prepared for the Boston Urban Observatory (August, 1974): 3.

9. See National Environmental Policy Act of 1969, 42 U.S.C., Section 4331 *et seq* (1970), and Sections 61 and 62, C.30, Massachusetts General Laws.

10. James A. Roberts, "Just What Is An Environmental Impact Statement?" *Urban Land* (May 1973): 11.

against blue-collar construction workers primarily concerned with jobs and wages.[11]

In the emotion-charged atmosphere of "to build or not to build" the fundamental issue determining the future of housing has become obscured—building and maintaining neighborhood confidence. Paradoxically, the federal assistance programs encouraged a negative bias in the general perception of urban neighborhoods. Distribution formulas like "poverty counted twice" rewarded the municipalities that most effectively poor-mouthed their stock. The media and the citizenry vied in which could find more need, blight, and deterioration, unwittingly broadcasting the image that urban areas were becoming disaster areas, needy of massive relief. As this text spells out, neighborhood confidence was exchanged for limited federal assistance. In hindsight, viewed through the maze of red tape attached to this assistance, this was a poor bargain since without neighborhood confidence lenders retreat and city services decline; as qualified buyers, persuaded by the rhetoric, look to the suburbs, the urban neighborhoods become easy prey for unscrupulous owners and the stage is set for rapid decay and exploitation. Neighborhood confidence must be the cornerstone of any housing policy, and city after city inadvertently sacrificed this priceless commodity in the game to obtain federal assistance.

CHAPTER THEMES

The several chapters of this book concentrate upon the two selected issues of housing quality and housing choice.

Chapter 2 introduces Boston as an illustrative case, giving the reader an overview of the housing situation in a large metropolis. After enumerating the strengths and weaknesses inherent in the current situation, the composition of Boston's housing is elaborated. Readers who would be reluctant to accept the analyses and conclusions throughout this book without a rigorously erected data foundation are urged to turn to Appendix A, which provides the essential data upon which the inferences and conclusions in the main text are

11. Concern that the Massachusetts Environmental Policy Act of 1973 would stifle private development led to amendments of the law in 1974, Chapter 257, to ease perceived and actual burdens of the scope of the legislation and of its reporting procedures and requirements. Among the amendments were provisions exempting environmental impact reports for private projects from approval by the state secretary of environmental affairs, although the latter can submit comments on such reports to public agencies granting permit determinations, orders or other action authorizing the projects.

based. It takes a close look at the city's people, the neighborhoods they live in, and the shelter they occupy. It cites trends and patterns which have particular implications for housing needs, demands, and policies, analyzing factors of strength and weakness and gives special attention to indicators of income and racial disparities of population in the central city and the metropolitan area.

Chapter 3 is an effort to probe and raise the reader's understanding of neighborhood housing markets and the micro-dynamics affecting housing quality. It assigns neighborhoods to different categories based on existing housing conditions and market strengths and weaknesses. Using this typology as a frame of reference, the chapter illustrates how to apply the typology by developing housing/neighborhood maintenance and revitalization strategies for Boston's existing housing stock. Most readers will see this typology as the crux of the "new planning" with its stress on neighborhood perceptions and market factors as critical elements in interpreting the "hard" data and statistics on which the more traditional planning was based.

Chapter 4 proposes citywide housing and residential improvement strategies, focusing on the need to review lending practices, reform the property tax system, and restructure the municipal housing regulatory systems, if the goal of improved housing quality is to be attained. Readers concerned with bank lending practices and "redlining" will find this chapter of particular interest. It focuses on the value of mortgage disclosure, evaluates the impact of alleged restrictions on mortgage availability, and develops some measures for improved residential credit. Necessary changes in the administration of the city's taxation and regulatory functions to curb tax and "red tape blight" are also addressed.

Chapter 5 deals with the much more controversial issue: institutionalized inequities that relate to income and race within the Boston metropolitan area and within the central city. After describing prevailing patterns of disparity within metropolitan Boston —municipal tax service disparities, school disparities, private housing investment and lending disparities—Chapter 5 discusses a scheme of expanded housing opportunities which combines new construction and rehabilitation based on the realities of housing conditions and markets. This proposal takes into account the several forces contributing to these existing inequities and sets forth the type and extent of changes required to reduce them. It also suggests counterpart housing/neighborhood strategies to reduce disparities among neighborhoods within the city of Boston without sacrificing the priority needs of existing residents.

The final chapter of this book relates the considerations raised by the separate goals of improving quality and reducing disparities, in effect summarizing and evaluating where to go from here. The chapter indentifies the significant shifts in the federal, state, and local responsibilities that are occurring as well as what the public sector can actually do. The policy considerations generated throughout the body of this report are summarized and restated .here as tempered by these realities. For many readers, this chapter is the place to begin.

Chapter 2

An Overview of Boston's Housing Environment

Policy initiatives in housing and community development appear to be shifting from Washington to state capitols and city halls. The roles of the city in determining such policies will become increasingly important. If any city hall is to take full advantage of this imminent opportunity to make and shape housing policy, its officials require useful data on residents, their existing shelter, and future housing needs. Examining the analysis of population and housing in Boston, provided in Appendix A, it becomes apparent the city faces a number of basic decisions for the future. The housing environment has undergone significant changes over the last several decades, and there are both new forces at work as well as continuing conflicts and difficulties. Change and intervention require careful consideration and time to proceed. "Economic and social forces in urban areas are *not* self-balancing."[1] If decisions are not made consciously, then choices will occur by default.

This chapter provides detailed background on the city's housing picture. Emphasis throughout the discussion is on the fact that housing in the city is part of a changing and dynamic market. Moreover, Boston is a community with a wide range of neighborhoods. Only as housing strategies are designed and applied specifically to those separate neighborhoods can there be a real hope for success. The several dimensions of neighborhood housing dynamics and the impact they have on the choice of appropriate housing strategies are presented in the following chapter.

1. Daniel P. Moynihan, essay entitled, "Toward a National Urban Policy," *The Public Interest*, No. 17 (Fall 1969): 9–10.

FACTORS OF STRENGTH

1. Major shifts in population, employment, and income in Boston, as well as changes in life styles, have altered the composition and thus the needs of the city's housing consumers. The loss of manufacturing jobs in the 1950s has been offset by the services revolution which has brought a large flow of upgraded jobs to Boston, but two out of three of the new jobs have gone to suburbanites.

2. The population decline of the 1950s, a part of the nationwide exodus of middle-income families to the suburbs, slowed down in the 1960s, and population levels since 1970 have stabilized and seem to be rising modestly. In the first several years of the seventies there has been an upward population trend, particularly in the 25–34 year old group, many of whom are young professionals who both work in the city and are interested in the life style and amenities the central city supports.

3. Resident ownership is still high in the city. As of 1970 approximately 71 percent of all residential structures had the owner living in them. Among small structures containing four or fewer units, the degree of owner occupancy was 77 percent.

4. Overall household incomes in Boston (in constant dollars) rose by almost one-fourth during the decade of the sixties. A new middle class is being created, giving rise to a growing demand for new and upgraded housing, after years in which the city increasingly served as a haven for the old, the poor, and students.

5. In the process, Boston's housing stock is being upgraded in a number of areas through new construction and renovation, and the demolition of obsolescent buildings. An expanded level of city expenditures for public facilities and capital improvements is encouraging this process.

COMPETING PROBLEMS

1. Conflicts often arise when rising demand raises rents of existing units, forcing tenants to pay more or face displacement. For example, in the South End, in Charlestown, and to some extent in the North End, there is tension between older residents and more affluent newcomers.

2. Although household incomes in Boston rose in the sixties, 17 percent of Boston's households still reported incomes in the 1970 census which were below the poverty level—incomes which often are inadequate to meet the cost of decent housing services and maintenance without subsidies—and the income discrepancy between Bos-

ton residents and their neighbors in the metropolitan area has continued to widen.

3. The elderly comprise a significant proportion of the city's population (12.7 percent in 1970), a proportion which has increased over the past decade. In addition, 35 percent of all one- to four-unit, owner-occupied housing structures in Boston were owned by persons over 62 years of age in 1970. Who will replace these resident owners as they pass on is uncertain and problematic. In the past tenants often became the owners, but more recently, fewer and fewer tenants have qualified for mortgages, barring them from resident ownership.

4. The city continues to house a disproportionate share of the lower income population, as well as the racial minorities living in the metropolitan area, thereby exacerbating the socioeconomic imbalance between the central city and the suburb.

5. The uncertainties attending federally-mandated busing and court-ordered 100 percent property revaluation have slowed the demand for housing coming on the market, which, in turn, gives current owners a feeling of being locked in or unable to sell their property at fair market value.

6. Although housing disinvestment and abandonment is not yet a major problem in Boston, there are some limited areas with very weak effective housing demand where ownership is shifting to absentees. Although the abandonment rate is under 1 percent per annum, weak demand currently affects one-sixth of the housing stock.

7. Bank red-lining, the restricted availability of mortgages and home improvement loans, has become a major issue affecting residents in many sound and stable sections of the city, as well as those in obvious pockets of decline. Whether changing lending practices, slackening desire to buy in Boston, or real estate broker practices underlie these serious changes in effective demand is uncertain, but increased understanding and resolution of the lending pinch is rapidly becoming the prime issue affecting Boston's existing housing.

8. The impact of rent control on housing maintenance and investment is frequently cited as the cause of deterioration. There clearly were speculative investments made in housing during the 1960s, and rising interest rates have wiped these out even in non-rent controlled communities. But few foresaw the impact of permanent rent control and rapidly inflating operating costs on housing investment. Widespread disinvestment threatens unless rents and operating costs are brought into a predictable and controlled relationship.

9. Finally, there have also been changes in the ability of the city to cope with the diverse housing needs presented by its population. Escalating costs of construction and maintenance, high interest rates, and the difficulty in obtaining mortgage and home improvement money threaten the city's aging housing stock in some areas. In addition, plans for new housing have been slowed in some neighborhoods of the city and there are forces which are hostile to new residential developments as demonstrated by community opposition, resistance to high-rise development, and public requirements for environmental protection.

10. At the same time, the federal role in housing is completely altered from a few years ago. The federal moratorium on many housing related programs, instituted in 1972, left Boston with major uncertainty regarding its traditional system of "remedies"— urban renewal, federally-assisted code enforcement and renovation, and subsidized private and public housing construction. HUD's shift to Community Development Block Grants and Sec. 8 Housing Assistance coupled with limited experimentation in new housing strategies such as housing allowances have given the city more discretion but radically less resources in planning for its future.

The factors of strength and the problems outlined above have brought the city to an important crossroad regarding housing policy. It is not sufficient to call for renewed allocations to finance the programs of the past, many of which require serious rethinking. Rather, the city of Boston decided in 1972 the time was ripe for a comprehensive review of its own housing needs, policies, and priorities. In the past, responses to changes in the housing market have generally been met in a piecemeal fashion, and there has been a tendency for various actors to pull in competing directions. It is unrealistic to think that this will change radically, but there is a need for a coordinated policy and program which will provide a framework for discussion and action. The key to such a policy lies in formulating and implementing strategies which complement and leverage the private market—encouraging owners, tenants, and lenders to play constructive roles in maintaining and improving Boston's existing housing and replacing obsolescent dwellings for new needs and demands.

COMPOSITION OF BOSTON'S HOUSING STOCK

Boston's housing stock covers a wide spectrum of housing styles and types. Within this spectrum there are very distinct characteris-

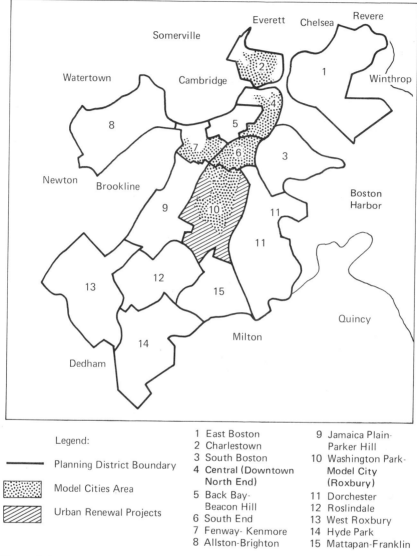

Legend:

――― Planning District Boundary

▨ Model Cities Area

▨ Urban Renewal Projects

1 East Boston
2 Charlestown
3 South Boston
4 Central (Downtown North End)
5 Back Bay- Beacon Hill
6 South End
7 Fenway- Kenmore
8 Allston-Brighton

9 Jamaica Plain- Parker Hill
10 Washington Park- Model City (Roxbury)
11 Dorchester
12 Roslindale
13 West Roxbury
14 Hyde Park
15 Mattapan-Franklin

Figure 2-1. Map of Boston Showing 1970 Planning Districts

tics that overshadow any general description of that stock. Consequently, a brief summary of these characteristics will be useful in understanding the nature of housing in Boston.

According to the 1970 U.S. Census there were 232,000 units distributed within 81,000 structures in the city of Boston. While single-family residences do not comprise a great percentage of either structures or units, most of the stock is comprised of smaller build-

ings, that is, buildings with six or fewer units, (and primarily two-
and three-unit buildings). These buildings represent 97 percent
of all the structures and contain 67 percent of all the units in the
city. Over three-quarters of the units were over thirty years old in
1970 and a good proportion of these were built before the turn of
the century.[2] The great majority of buildings in Boston and almost
all of those with six or less units are of frame construction. The remaining one-third of the city's units are largely in structures of
masonry construction.

The nature of the housing stock has changed comparatively little
in recent decades, but the characteristics of its residents have changed
considerably. The city recently experienced a major influx of young
adults. This trend towards both an increasingly elderly and young
adult population resulted in a drop in average household size to
2.8 persons while the median number of rooms per dwelling unit
was 5.2. Overall, this indicates that there is adequate room for most
households. However, in many neighborhoods where demand has
been strong—notably Allston-Brighton, Back Bay-Beacon Hill, and
Charlestown—there have been conversions, both legal and illegal,
from large units to smaller ones.[3] On the other hand, 7.6 percent of
Boston's occupied units were classified as overcrowded in 1970.[4]
Still, when compared with overcrowding in the Boston SMSA or in
other central cities nationwide, Boston's rate is not serious.[5]

Major Structure Types

Based on an analysis of the 1971 tax assessing records for the city;
an even more complete description of the city's housing can be provided. Initially, it is possible to classify Boston's housing into three
structural categories:

1. *masonry structures* generally built either before the turn of the
   century, or in the 1920s;
2. *wood frame structures* built from 1850 on, but with the majority

2. As would be expected, the housing stock in Boston is older than that of its
neighbors in the SMSA. In 1970, according to the Census, with 26 percent of
the area's units, Boston accounted for 32 percent of those built before 1940,
but only 14 percent of those built in 1969.

3. The financial advantages of conversions to investors (two small units are
more profitable than one large unit) has led, in areas of strong demand by young
persons, to the displacement of renting families.

4. An overcrowded unit is one which houses 1.01 or more person per room.

5. For the Boston SMSA, the 1970 overcrowding rate was 5.7; for all SMSAs
in the nation, it was 7.7; for all central cities it was 8.5; for the entire nation it
was 8.2.

constructed from the turn of the century through a construction boom in the 1920s; and

3. *post-1930s multi-family and apartment construction.*

In general terms, 64 percent of Boston's housing units are wood frame, with about 20 percent being brick masonry, and the other 16 percent being in postwar construction. Within each general category, though, there are a number of important differences and variations which require explanation.

Brick Masonry. The brick masonry structures can be divided into major groupings. The first (comprising about 30,000 dwelling units) is made up primarily of brick row houses and town houses found in Beacon Hill, the South End, Back Bay, Charlestown, and in isolated parts of other neighborhoods including Roxbury, East Boston, and Dorchester Heights (Telegraph Hill). As the city of Boston evolved, most of these areas served their turn as the most fashionable part of the city.

Each of these areas, then, consisted of solidly-built, quality housing marketed for the upper-income residents of the city. As markets, tastes, and income patterns shifted, most of those areas have seen changes in resident composition as the original resident class moved on to be replaced by a progression of residents possessing differing incomes, class, ethnic, and sometimes racial backgrounds. As this process continued, most of the areas have experienced a marked decline in demand at one time or another. However, as tastes and incomes again change, some areas have already seen a resurgence of demand. Thus, some areas, such as Back Bay and Beacon Hill, have already seen rehabilitation and revival, while others, such as the South End and Charlestown, are presently undergoing that same process of new demand and physical upgrading.

The second major building type within the brick masonry classification is the larger, more dense apartment buildings constructed mainly during the post-World War I housing boom. These buildings were originally constructed for a fairly solid, middle-class constituency and are concentrated primarily in southern Brighton, Allston, the Fenway, along Huntington Avenue, and major arterials in Roxbury, Jamaica Plain, and Dorchester. There are approximately 15,000 of these units today, housing a wide variety of the city's population, including students, elderly, and low-income families. Consequently, these units reflect a broad range in terms of maintenance and physical condition.

A final small subgroup of masonry structures are found in the North End, Chinatown, and parts of South Cove. Most of these buildings were originally built before the turn of the century and served as tenement-style housing for many of the city's new immigrant groups. In terms of categories, they are probably closer to the first brick masonry classification. Although the first two still house tightly-knit, ethnic communities, demand is strong due to their location, colorful environments and historical signficance.

Wood Frame. Wood frame structures comprise nearly two-thirds (64 percent of all units) of the city's housing stock. Such construction is generally found throughout the city with the exception of the more close-in areas (which generally consist of the brick masonry structures discussed previously).

Of this wood frame stock, almost all (95 percent) are in triple-decker, two-family, and more recently, single-family structures. The great majority of these buildings are occupied by resident owners today, although some are quite elderly.

The first major subgroup is the triple deckers, a unique and important part of Boston's housing stock. With the exception of West Roxbury, they are found in large numbers in almost all parts of wood-frame Boston, including such neighborhoods as East Boston, South Boston, and Charlestown. The boom for constructing these buildings came between 1880 and 1914 and, in part, was precipitated by a new building code established after the Great Boston Fire in 1872. They were originally marketed for lower-middle-class and middle-class families (thus reflecting a variety of quality, detailing, and styles) seeking turn of the century "suburbia" which the advent of the streetcar put within their reach. These structures quickly filled up most previously undeveloped land within reach. Furthermore, with two income-producing units, it made home ownership available for the first time to a new and broader class of Bostonians.

Today, triple deckers contain a quarter of all units and comprise 24 percent of the wood-frame structures in Boston. They reflect a wide variety of conditions (from complete modernization to abandonment), rent levels, and styles of ownership as they have been impacted by change within the individual neighborhoods in which they are found. However, they are still largely owner-occupied (over 60 percent) as their size and construction (frame) do not present the maintenance and management advantages of the larger brick buildings to investor owners.

The single-family houses, on the other hand, are generally the most recently constructed of the frame housing subgroups, and therefore, are mostly concentrated in the more recently built-up, outlying Boston neighborhoods (Roslindale, Hyde Park, West Roxbury, and southern Dorchester). Others are scattered throughout the remainder of Boston, having originally been built by the privileged as residences "out in the country." In total, single families make up 14 percent of Boston's housing stock (by units) and 42 percent of all wood-frame structures.

Two-family houses follow largely the same pattern as single families in regards to location and resident ownership (85 percent vs. 90 percent for singles). Most were built during the 1920s housing boom while single-family houses span a much longer range in time—from the Victorian era to the present. Two families represent a 16 percent share of the total housing units—slightly more than the single families—but account for only 30 percent of wood-frame structures. As a group, wood-frame structures present more problems than the brick in terms of preservation and rehabilitation. Most of the brick neighborhoods are close in and have already experienced periods of being very much in fashion, as well as other times when they were out of fashion. This "trial by blight" is just in the process of being applied to the frame stock, which is clearly more vulnerable to poor maintenance, misuse and abuse by tenants and landlords, and general neighborhood disinvestment. Properly maintained and cared for, however, the typical frame structures can last indefinitely, and at much lower monthly costs than any conceivable replacement construction. To be cost effective, city housing policy must be focused on preserving this stock and preventing neglect, rather than restoring seriously deteriorated structures and attempting to overcome the effects of years of neglect.

Post-1930s Multi-Family and Apartment Construction. While these buildings are of considerably higher density than previous construction, they vary widely as to their market (and thereby, rent levels), location, financing, and period of primary construction. Within this group there are four major components of building types—public housing, garden apartments, high-rise apartments, and developments built under mortgage subsidy plans. Although this category consists of only 16 percent of the housing stock, it is largely rental housing and includes the great majority of all construction in Boston since the depression.[6] (The only other significant residential construction during this period has been single-family

---

6. Condominiums are not yet statistically significant in Boston.

homes during periods of prosperity, discussed under frame structures above).

Almost all large-scale public housing projects were constructed in Boston between 1940 and 1954. Since then, construction has been oriented towards smaller-scale developments and aiding the elderly, bringing the total number of public housing units today to 16,147 or 7 percent of the housing stock. These units house predominantly lower-income families clustered in locations throughout many parts of the city.

Garden-type apartments have been built largely in the 1950s and 1960s and make up an approximate 10,000 units or 4 percent of the housing stock. Unlike public housing, which covers a relatively broad range of neighborhoods, garden-type apartments are limited to the outlying, middle-class neighborhoods, such as West Roxbury, Hyde Park, Roslindale, and Allston-Brighton. This distribution is attributable to both the availability of undeveloped land during this period and the location of the middle-class market demand at the time they were conceived.

The third class of postwar structures consists of high-rise buildings. These have been constructed largely since 1960 and are concentrated in choice locations near the Downtown areas of Boston. Approximately 5,000 of these units exist in Boston today, mostly in the luxury class.

The last category is that of subsidized construction. This type of construction was a result of the Federal Housing Programs of the late 1960s and early 1970s, which subsidized mortgage interest rates for the private development of low- and moderate-income projects. The state through the Massachusetts Housing Finance Agency (MHFA) also has made small additions to this class of buildings. Altogether, a total of 17,486 (or 8 percent of the housing stock) of these federally and state subsidized units now exist, many of which are concentrated in a few inner-city neighborhoods— namely Roxbury and the South End.

In summary, postwar construction has taken place in most Boston neighborhoods, but at different times, and for different income classes. Prior to 1966, the bulk of new construction had been privately financed with the exception of public housing which had been built over a relatively long time span. However, since 1966, this has shifted markedly towards subsidized construction as Boston vigorously pursued available federal and state programs. This increased dependence on subsidies which have now been curtailed raises a new challenge for Boston: how to promote a continuing flow of new residential construction.

Chapter 3

Neighborhood Revitalization Strategies

This chapter focuses on housing conditions and market trends in Boston to develop conservation and revitalization strategies appropriate to the city's various housing market situations. Since humanistic planning seeks to use public resources for stimulating private investment as far as possible, public programs must be tailored to neighborhood dynamics, not simply applied where the need seems greatest. The chapter develops a framework for estimating the additional public outlays required to eliminate substandard housing conditions in a lasting manner. It outlines actions required at the neighborhood, municipal, state, and federal levels, but places emphasis on programs applicable to the neighborhood level.

The chapter begins with an examination of current housing conditions and the costs of fix-up necessary to bring housing up to minimum code standards, and continues with a discussion of housing dynamics before identifying and sorting out appropriate public responses. The chapter that follows complements these proposals for neighborhood strategies and tactics with recommended city-wide initiatives for housing preservation.

APPRAISING HOUSING CONDITIONS

The condition of Boston's housing stock compares favorably with the inventory of most northeastern central cities. While there are pockets of severe deterioration, these are limited and scattered, posing no threat of domino-like blight sweeping over extensive sections.

Compared to the surrounding suburbs, Boston's stock is older, but many sections contain prized, brick front row-houses, early frame dwellings or impressive Victorian edifices and carriage houses which often lend prestige to the surrounding neighborhood. In other sections there are similar opportunities to enhance neighborhoods by focusing on architectural assets and locational advantages that few of the surrounding suburbs share.

However, signs of neglect are evident; and although neighborhood revitalization is being given new priority throughout much of the city, it is important to discover means of effective early intervention before fix-up becomes more costly and confidence in particular neighborhoods wanes.

A more thorough knowledge of housing conditions and market dynamics form the starting point for effective housing preservation. To develop some standards for judging housing conditions, the research staff of the BRA joined rehabilitation specialists of the city's Housing Inspection Department in 1973 in developing indices of housing quality as measured by the varying amounts of resources required to bring units up to the city minimum code standards.[1] The continuum of required resource levels has been partitioned somewhat arbitrarily into five commonly used descriptions of upgrading levels.

The first category, "A," includes dwellings which are presently in good condition or for which a minimal amount of repair, not exceeding $500, is necessary to bring the property up to code.[2] The second category, "B," includes housing for which a modest amount of work, not exceeding $1,000, would be sufficient. Category "C" includes units which have code violations serious enough to qualify them for federally-assisted code enforcement (FACE) programs. Units within this group generally require the replacement of a major system—

1. There are no universally accepted definitions of housing quality. U.S. Bureau of the Census indicators of housing quality in 1970 are inadequate. For example, the commonly accepted proxy for quality, units lacking one or more plumbing facilities, shows that these units are concentrated in the Central, Beacon Hill, North End, South End and East Boston stock, i.e., the oldest stock. These are *not* the areas with the most seriously deteriorated housing.

2. All estimates are in 1973 dollars and have been costed out on a *per unit* basis, even though conditions generally affect the stock structure by structure. These fix-up costs are based on prices in a private market situation where subcontractors are dealt with directly, by owners acting in self interest and do not include allowances for recurring maintenance such as painting. At present an owner can "gut rehabilitate" units for less than $10,000, provided he owns the building, it is in fair structural shape, and he is not required to hire and train unskilled persons, obtain the consent of community groups and the like. In other words these costs are *not* to be compared with rehabilitation costs under federal housing programs such as Section 236.

electrical, plumbing, or heating—costing $1,000 to $3,000. Category "D" refers to housing for which gut rehabilitation, with a cost ranging from $3,000 to $10,000 per dwelling is the only solution. Finally, category "E" includes those units for which fix-up would not be feasible at all, and which should be demolished.

The entire housing stock of the city has been evaluated in light of this descriptive scheme.[3] Table 3-1 provides a breakdown of this survey for each of the city's planning districts. In general terms, 31 percent of the city's units may be considered "good as is" (category A), and when added to those in category "B," the proportion of what are basically satisfactory dwellings reaches 70 percent. In other words, over two out of three dwellings require only limited assistance to meet basic code standards.[4] Units in category "C" comprise 24 percent of the housing stock. Approximately 5 percent of the stock is in bad enough condition to require gut rehabilitation; and 1 percent of the city's housing, essentially made up of units that have already been abandoned, requires demolition.

To give the reader a better feel for the locational aspects of housing condition in Boston, Figure 3-1 illustrates the geographic distribution of those units which are in the worst condition, either requiring gut rehabilitation or demolition. The highest requirements for fix-up are found in Roxbury and parts of the South End, in the transitional areas of western Dorchester, in the older, ethnic areas of South and East Boston, and in the inner core. Some of these are the same areas where abandonments have occurred in the city, particularly in such areas as western Dorchester and Franklin Field where the BBURG[5] program in the late 1960s has resulted in widespread bank foreclosures with many of the mortgages going to HUD. Areas with high fix-up needs roughly coincide with areas in the city

3. Rehabilitation specialists from the Housing Inspection Department examined all residential areas outside of urban renewal areas and conducted exterior inspections of one-third of this stock. Their experience with this type of housing, gained from handling work write-ups and rehabilitation supervision under Boston's federally-assisted code enforcement program, has shown which exterior clues are associated with interior deficiencies, viz, outside wiring connections reveal whether the structure is wired "up to code." For urban renewal areas, Boston Redevelopment Authority data was examined within the framework of this same methodology.

4. The presence of lead-based paint was not such a critical issue at the time of the survey and should be separated from other dimensions of housing deterioration. Virtually any structure built before 1950 (i.e., most of the housing in Boston, Cambridge, and the close-in suburbs) contains lead paint. Costs and techniques for removing this hazard vary with the particular structure, but average at least $1,000 per dwelling, exceeding over a quarter of a billion dollars for the affected stock in Boston alone.

5. The Boston Banks Urban Renewal Group program was an assigned risk mortgage pool, discussed in detail on page 41 and on page 62.

Table 3-1. Housing Units by Conditions, City of Boston, 1973

Planning District	Total Units	A: %	$250 #	B: %	$750 #	Condition[1] C: %	$2,000 #	D: %	$8,000 #	E: %	Demolition #	Per Unit Fix-Up Cost[2]
East Boston	13,575	17	2,276	37	4,996	39	5,358	6	797	1	148	$1,577
Charlestown	5,371	28	1,484	30	1,635	40	2,146	2	94	—	12	1,237
South Boston	14,739	21	3,012	39	5,951	31	4,434	8	1,086	2	256	1,577
West End	1,490	67	998	22	328	10	149	1	15	—	—	613
North End	4,251	36	1,528	35	1,472	20	838	10	413	—	—	1,521
South Cove	959	49	472	31	297	17	162	3	28	—	—	927
Central	1,615	35	570	19	311	22	353	23	372	1	9	2,513
Total	8,315	43	3,568	29	2,408	18	1,502	10	828	—	9	1,482
Back Bay/Beacon Hill	17,178	41	6,973	37	6,408	20	3,374	2	410	—	13	965
South End	10,771	17	1,846	29	3,165	45	4,892	7	731	1	137	1,715
Fenway/Kenmore	13,826	30	4,113	39	5,368	27	3,728	4	559	—	58	1,228
Allston/Brighton	25,319	41	10,491	41	10,353	17	4,256	1	219	—	—	816
Jamaica Plain/Parker Hill	16,227	33	5,377	39	6,371	24	3,858	3	444	1	177	1,072
Washington Park	7,161	29	2,065	35	2,541	24	1,747	11	763	1	45	1,679
Model City	17,209	11	1,970	31	5,291	32	5,498	21	3,604	5	846	2,574
Campus High	842	1	6	9	76	45	381	34	286	11	93	3,692
Total	25,212	16	4,041	31	7,908	30	7,626	19	4,653	4	984	2,357
Dorchester 1	10,470	21	2,217	47	4,879	30	3,133	2	211	1	30	1,162
Dorchester 2	23,140	20	4,579	52	12,010	26	5,951	2	461	1	139	1,112
Mattapan	14,947	22	3,240	50	7,442	20	3,001	7	1,030	2	234	1,380
Total	48,557	21	10,036	50	24,331	25	12,085	4	1,702	1	403	1,207
Roslindale	12,005	49	5,827	44	5,280	7	819	1	77	—	2	639
West Roxbury	11,022	70	7,724	28	3,049	2	249	—	—	—	—	428
Hyde Park	10,738	50	5,384	39	4,152	9	949	2	225	—	28	760
City Totals	232,856	31	72,152	39	91,375	24	55,276	5	11,826	1	2,227	1,253

1. "Condition" is expressed as an average per unit cost of fix-up to code standards.
2. This is a weighted average which excludes units in Category E (which should be demolished rather than fixed up.)

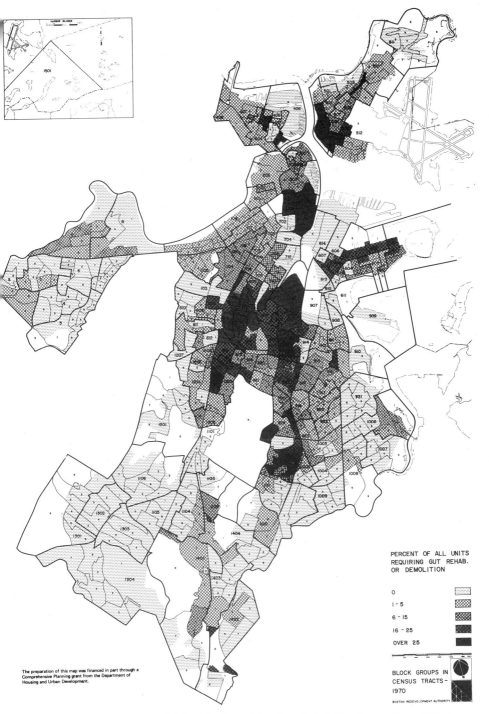

The preparation of this map was financed in part through a
Comprehensive Planning grant from the Department of
Housing and Urban Development.

PERCENT OF ALL UNITS
REQUIRING GUT REHAB.
OR DEMOLITION

0

1 - 5

6 - 15

16 - 25

OVER 25

BLOCK GROUPS IN
CENSUS TRACTS -
1970

BOSTON REDEVELOPMENT AUTHORITY

Figure 3-1. Percentage of All Units Requiring Gut Rehabilitation or Demolition

Table 3-2.   Estimated Total Fix-up Costs by Private Means

Condition	Number of Units	Percentage of Stock	Per Unit Cost of Fix-Up by Private Means	Total Cost of Fix-Up by Private Means
A	72,152	(31)	$ 250	$ 18,038,000
B	91,375	(39)	$ 750	$ 68,532,000
C	55,276	(24)	$2,000	$110,556,000
D	11,826	(5)	$8,000	$ 94,592,000
Sub Total	230,629			$291,718,000
E	2,227	(1)	demolish	
Total	232,856			

where incomes are low and, therefore, represent areas where it will be difficult to spur fix-up without some form of public subsidy.

Translating condition into rehabilitation costs, table 3-2 gives the cost of fix-up by private means to substantial code compliance in each of the categories excepting demolition.[6] Whether such private incentives are present and how they could be activated is the focus of the next section below.

Figure 3-2 illustrates the variation in average fix-up work by neighborhoods, suggesting the level of effort required to bring all the stock in each one into code compliance.[7]

In summary, two-thirds of the stock requires only limited assistance, averaging under $600 per unit, to achieve substantial code compliance. Another quarter of the stock requires an average of $2,000 per unit, leaving a residual 14,000 units or one-eighteenth of the stock. At the time of the condition survey, it was thought that the majority of these 14,000 units could be "gut rehabilitated" if private market incentives could be devised, but as yet, this has not occurred. These seriously deteriorated structures are expensive to rehabilitate. The city faces the choice of using the limited available resources to leverage private investment and stabilize thousands of units, or to directly meet the capital costs of restor-

6. The cost of demolition (category E) is not included. $1,000 per unit or $2,227,000 would be required for the necessary demolitions. Due to the location of virtually all these units in zones of abandonment, this would necessarily be a public cost. Note that only 11,824 units in category D (less than 5 percent of the city stock) would cost over $94 million, or nearly one-third of the total fix-up cost. It is much more cost-effective to intervene while structures are in the category C or better.

7. Estimated fix-up costs for individual structures were averaged for the stock type within each census block group and then a weighted average fix-up cost was derived. The costs of particular structures often vary widely around this average.

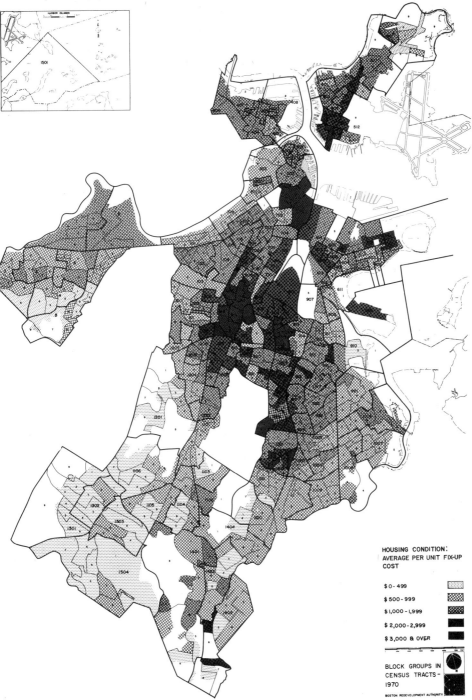

HOUSING CONDITION:
AVERAGE PER UNIT FIX-UP
COST

$ 0 - 499

$ 500 - 999

$ 1,000 - 1,999

$ 2,000 - 2,999

$ 3,000 & OVER

BLOCK GROUPS IN
CENSUS TRACTS -
1970

BOSTON REDEVELOPMENT AUTHORITY

Figure 3-2. Housing Condition: Average Per Unit Fix-up Cost

29

ing a few hundred units. The entire fix-up task, requiring close to $300 million requires setting priorities. To aid in setting such priorities requires a closer look at neighborhood housing dynamics.

NEIGHBORHOOD MARKET DYNAMICS

The condition of the housing, although sometimes illusive, is a "hard" indicator of the health of the housing stock which can be measured and quantified. However, it is also necessary to examine another dimension of residential health which is often more difficult to define, the strength of the housing market—the balance between the number of households trying to move into, stay, and leave an area. Measurement of market dynamics is more difficult. An analysis of objective data such as changes in housing sales values, rent levels, and vacancy rates only reflect these perceptions after a time lag. More subjective observations, such as attitudes of lenders, realtors, city agencies, owners, and residents must be probed to gauge market dynamics. Perceptions of an area as a strong or weak real estate investment will elicit widely different actions in regard to housing maintenance, upgrading, and sale or purchase.[8]

Techniques for measuring market strength are still somewhat underdeveloped and primitive, but this dimension is critical to arriving at effective housing strategies. Strong market areas mean there are more applicants than vacancies, or more households who wish to live in the neighborhood than there are available dwelling units. In stable neighborhoods, supply and demand balance out, whereas in weak market areas there are fewer households seeking to remain than available dwellings. As an illustration of how strategies should be tailored to housing market strength consider code enforcement: while appropriate and effective in strong and stable markets, code enforcement in weak market areas can be counterproductive, spurring disinvestment and even abandonment. Neighborhoods throughout the city have been tentatively located on this market strength spectrum.[9] Examination of the map of housing condition data (see

8. Price appreciation is often taken as a sign of a strong housing market, and abandonment of an extremely weak one. But years of countless interactions precede abandonment or a new uptrend. Housing policy must be attuned to influencing these interactions to prevent disinvestment or speculative abuses.

9. The BRA Research and Planning staff have collaborated in this effort drawing on both hard data sources (mortgage sales, vacancy rates, etc.) and experience with many of the actors in the real estate industry (including owners, tenants, brokers, lenders, other public officials, etc.). Awareness of the sensitivity of these trends to "self-fulfilling prophecies" prevents publication of the individual neighborhood rankings.

fig. 3-2—revealed that areas in similar conditions are subject to very different market influences, and further that there are areas with poor conditions in a very strong market (South End) as well as areas in fair to good condition but with a weak housing market where owners of essentially sound houses are disinvesting because they fear a lack of qualified buyers may result from possible neighborhood change. By examining the change in black occupancy from 1960 to 1970, one obtains a hint of where some of these dynamics are operating (see fig. 3-3 and 3-4). To be effective, city policy must become attuned to subtler differentiations and devise means of affecting neighborhood confidence rather than simply restoring deteriorating houses.

A matrix results from combining the housing condition dimension with the market perception dimension (see fig. 3-5). Each neighborhood can be located within the resulting conceptual framework, shown as figure 3-6, which identifies some of the symptoms associated with different types of neighborhoods.[10] The cost of maintaining and upgrading is a function of condition; but the incentive to do so depends in many cases on the strength of housing demand and the change in market value resulting from upgrading. A market perceived by key actors as rising differs sharply from one seen as declining, and their futures, even for superficially similar neighborhoods with essentially the same housing condition, will differ widely.

Although various mortgage information sources, postal vacancy surveys, and the U.S. Census provide limited objective data on past market trends, turnover, and vacancy rates, this information proved to be inadequate because it failed to capture the influences on the investors. The opening of a new University of Massachusetts campus as well as the proposed JFK library nearby at Columbia Point in Dorchester are already perceived as reversing a long declining trend in adjoining neighborhoods by introducing new buyers, but hard evidence on the impact is still inconclusive. Similarly, some stable neighborhoods in Jamaica Plain may begin to decline because long-term resident owners are now quite elderly. It is likely that too many structures will come up for sale in the next decade compared to the current number of buyers. While imaginative interpretation of census data would have uncovered this inference, analysis of trend data cannot tell us whether an equal number of new buyers to balance sellers

10. For the sake of simplicity, the former categories of condition have been condensed, and *areas* of the city have been classified according to three levels of condition—good (housing needs at most minor repairs, such as exterior painting), moderate (housing needs moderate repairs, to deal with deferred maintenance), and serious (housing needs major repairs such as new mechanical systems, plumbing, and/or heating).

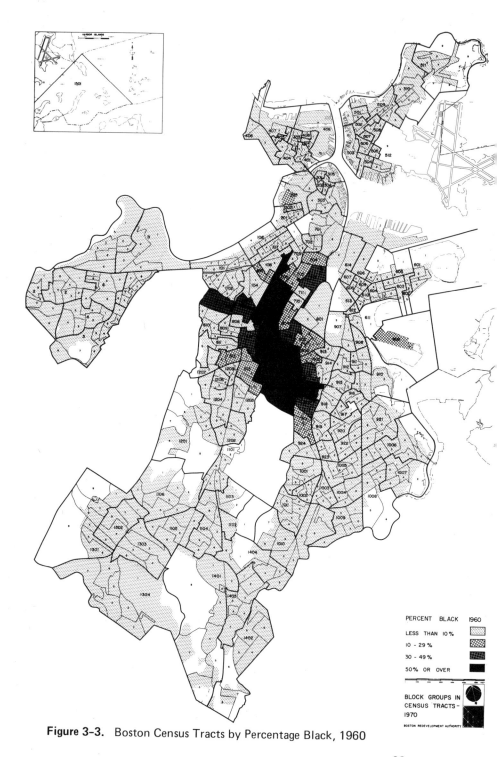

PERCENT BLACK 1960

LESS THAN 10 %

10 - 29 %

30 - 49 %

50 % OR OVER

BLOCK GROUPS IN
CENSUS TRACTS -
1970

BOSTON REDEVELOPMENT AUTHORITY

Figure 3-3. Boston Census Tracts by Percentage Black, 1960

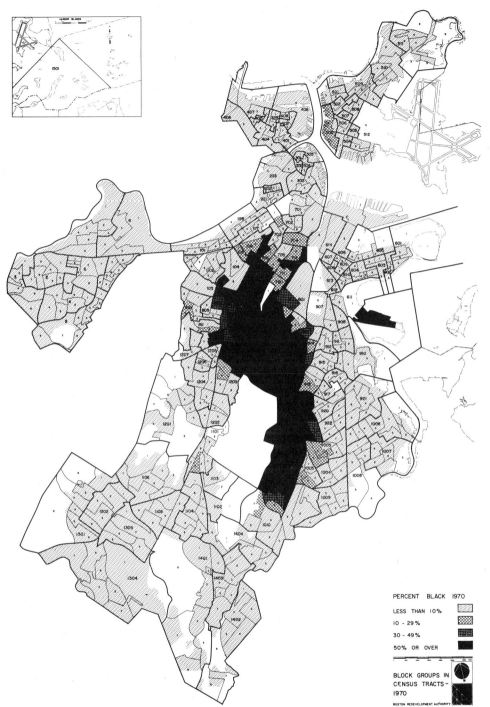

Figure 3-4. Boston Census Tracts by Percentage Black, 1970

33

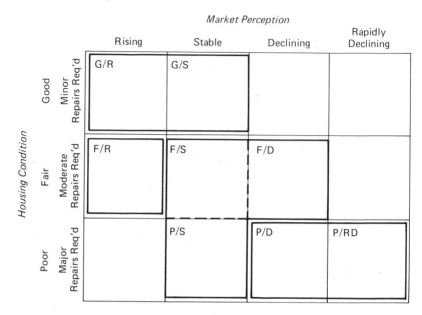

Figure 3-5. Conceptual Framework for Neighborhood Classification

will be available. Census data, mortgage trends, and countless interviews and impressions must be integrated in classifying each neighborhood. One clear correlation with declining demand emerged, but one difficult to obtain from conventionally available data: a reduction in gross rent multiplier—the ratio between market value and annual gross rent. It seems that resident owners keep rents modest to retain traditional tenants, but as effective demand slows and some of these structures come on the market, they are sold for less than before, and the new owners, usually absentees, charge more to a new set of tenants who are often partially on public assistance.[11]

Figure 3-7 shows the estimated percentage of the city's units which fall into each of the various neighborhood types, and figure 3-8 gives a rough approximation as to location.

11. In assessing market trends, the BRA planning and research staff pooled their efforts. 1960-1970 census data interpreted dynamically furnished the background. Interviews with brokers and lenders, as well as district planners' experience with community groups, furnished valuable clues, but the interpretation remains largely a subjective exercise. These appraisals are *consensus perceptions*, which can alter within a few years. They do not promise that an area will rise or decline in market value; they merely reflect the climate in which housing entrepreneurs in these neighborhoods are currently acting. There is, of course, the danger that the classification is self-fulfilling, that labeling an area as declining *causes* its decline; but this must be balanced against the dysfunctions of devising policy in ignorance.

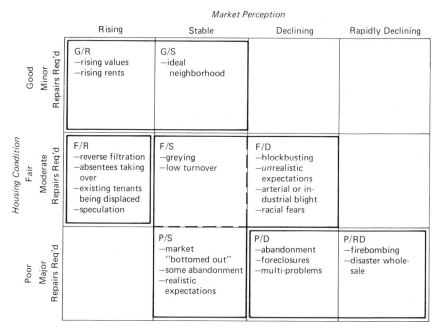

Figure 3-6. Neighborhood Characteristics Associated with Housing Market/ Condition Classifications

Housing policy, in the past, has always been based on the assumption that housing demand is equally effective in all neighborhoods. In fact, the incentive to invest in housing fix-up is not equally present in all neighborhoods. Only about half of Boston's stock is located in neighborhoods where housing supply and demand are in a state of balance, whereas one-third of the stock is affected by strong demand, that is, by forces where the number of prospective buyers and tenants exceed the opportunities coming on the market. On the other hand, one-sixth of the housing stock may be found in areas experiencing disinvestment, reflecting a weak and ineffective housing demand.[12]

12. As housing and especially heating and labor costs have escalated, many of Boston's less affluent households have been forced to spend increasing proportions of their income on housing. The majority of Boston residents are spending more than one-fourth of their income on housing and it is increasingly true that decent housing costs more than many households can afford to pay. Neighborhood blight tends to set in where too many such households with inadequate income become clustered and the area develops a stigma which adversely affects demand. This has occurred in some predominantly white low-income areas, but is more prevalent in neighborhoods where minorities are concentrated.

Market Perception

Housing Condition		Rising	Stable	Declining	Rapidly Declining	
Good Minor Repairs Req'd		G/R 15% 33,400 d.u.	G/S 17% 39,700 d.u.			32% 73,100 d.u.
Fair Moderate Repairs Req'd		F/R 21% 48,300 d.u.	F/S 23% 56,400 d.u.	F/D 6% 12,800 d.u.		50% 117,500 d.u.
Poor Major Repairs Req'd			P/S 9% 22,000 d.u.	P/D 8% 17,300 d.u.	P/RD 1% 1,600 d.u.	18% 40,900 d.u.
		36% 81,700 d.u.	49% 118,100 d.u.	14% 30,100 d.u.	1% 1,600 d.u.	

Figure 3-7. Dwelling Units and Percentage of Stock in Various Market/Condition Classes

Traditional housing programs are appropriate where demand and supply match; that is, they are suitable and adequate in themselves for about half of Boston's stock. Such innovations as homesteading, rehabilitation counseling, and special loan funds are also beneficial under these conditions. *But for the other half of the city's housing where supply and demand are in a state of imbalance, it is critical to determine whether demand exceeds supply or vice versa.* Where there is an excess of demand, the housing problems are likely to be spiralling rents caused by appreciation. Often owners refinance to capitalize or convert their increased equity into cash for other investments, and in this process tenants desiring to remain are required to pay more and more rent. If there is strong demand throughout a neighborhood, owners become tempted to convert or create additional dwelling units within existing structures to gain more rental income to meet their higher expenses and taxes. The casual observer may hear housing needs and shortages discussed in the same geographical area, but the underlying problem is likely to be speculation which is encouraged by the excessive demand for units in the area.

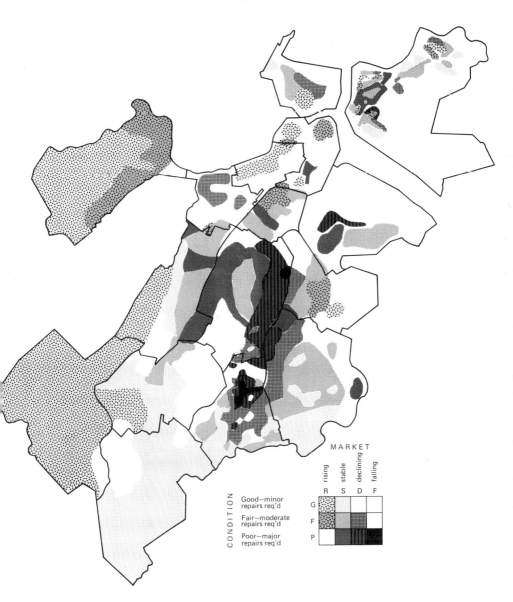

Figure 3-8. Neighborhood Classification by Market Dynamics and Condition

The most effective public policies in such cases are code enforcement, monitoring for illegal conversions, and rent control, to see that only operating cost increases are passed along, not the increased costs of financing generated by capitalization or appreciation.

In the declining areas, on the other hand, the problem is much more basic. Behind the confusing symptoms of neighborhood pathology—poorly maintained structures, scattered housing abandonment, and trash accumulation—is the lack of effective housing demand, the ability to afford the cost of decent housing. Whereas the rising neighborhoods are overattractive, declining neighborhoods are unattractive and the current residents tend frequently to compound the problem by "talking down" the area. As they "talk it down," they destroy confidence in the neighborhood and discourage whatever investments might otherwise have occurred. This causes an acceleration of the decline until it becomes contagious. Whereas disinvestment in some cities has become a devastating process, Boston is fortunately composed of highly variegated areas, thereby preventing a domino-effect loss of block after block of similar structures, a pattern that has occurred in widespread areas of other large cities. Declining areas in Boston are scattered, concentrated in pockets, and in the aggregate currently contain no more than one-sixth of the housing stock. The loss of confidence which pervades such neighborhoods, however, is a serious threat that can travel with disillusioned residents who abandon one area and shift into healthier areas unless adequate assistance is provided and care is taken to assure that confidence is not undermined in currently stable areas. One of the prime housing policy challenges confronting the city is to achieve this kind of support for disadvantaged households, instead of embarking on futile efforts to "gut rehabilitate" the areas these households currently occupy.

To better understand possible housing policy options appropriate to the various submarket situations requires a brief but critical review of past experience.

DRAWING INFERENCES FROM THE PAST EFFORTS TO DEVELOP GUIDELINES FOR FUTURE HOUSING

This section interprets past housing actions in light of the current conditions and trends in Boston's housing situation provided above, to develop a set of guiding principles for future housing policy.

Past Public Efforts

Within the last twenty years there have been four major areas of public interaction affecting housing: urban renewal; multifamily housing under various publicly-assisted development programs (like sec. 221(d)(3) and 236); federally-assisted code enforcement (under sec. 115 and 312); and the Boston Banks Urban Renewal Group home loan program. A brief discussion of each is appropriate.

Boston's urban renewal effort was the largest in the nation for a city of its size, bringing in an average of $37 million annually between 1969 and 1974, and reaching a peak of nearly $90 million in 1972 alone. The program was boldly conceived and supported an unprecedented office boom, provided sites for new government buildings and higher income housing along with construction of over 8,000 new units and a similar amount of rehabilitation for low- and moderate-income households, as well as numerous new public buildings in neighborhood renewal areas.

Within specifically defined renewal areas, ambitious plans were formulated for new housing development schemes and high targets were set for rehabilitation. Slightly more than half the new construction, but still less than half the rehabilitation has been completed.

The achievements are substantial, but the changes in federal funding have forced a realization that the costs of finishing the renewal plans have escalated out of reach. Not only is the anticipated flow of federal assistance under community development block grants inadequate to complete the planned renewal, but the durability of the completed housing is challenged by alarming rates of financial difficulty and reports of serious deterioration in many of the developments. At the same time, new areas are competing for assistance to curb blight and prevent neighborhood decline.

While there has been no rigorous evaluation of the overall impact of urban renewal, it seems clear that solving Boston's housing problems cannot be included among its tangible achievements. After over a decade of sustained effort, as much housing is in jeopardy today citywide as before, and urban renewal seems to have simply displaced or relocated most lower-income households in the process of reestablishing the middle class in some residential sections where lower-income households predominated in the early 1960s.

If we consider the high per-unit construction and operating costs of the replacement housing, the potential value of the demolished brick stock if the market context could have been altered, along with the trauma inflicted on the residents of areas undergoing the renewal, then the assumed net benefits of urban renewal are offset by many less tangible costs and opportunities foregone. In the future, there is undoubtedly a role for renewal and redevelopment, but not in occupied residential sections, even when blighted. Currently, attention has shifted from renewal to saving existing neighborhoods. Redevelopment will reemerge as a housing policy tool, but its applications must be more carefully considered and fine-tuned to factors that were misunderstood or ignored in the past.

Subsidized housing production, both new and rehab, will also remain an important tool, but where and how it is applied must be altered.

Over 15,000 subsidized units were built under Sec. 221(d)(3) and 236, and virtually all of these developments are experiencing sharply rising operating costs with little increase in revenues. Unless new forms of subsidies can be applied, foreclosures are inevitable, tarnishing subsidized development generally.

The developments sponsored by the Massachusetts Housing Finance Agency were more carefully screened and financially sounder at the outset, but inflation in operating expenses is gnawing at their positive cash flow as well.[13] Recent problems in marketing MHFA's tax-exempt bonds have compounded the constraints on additional subsidized housing development. As a result, the newest form of federal housing assistance, Sec. 8 leased housing (enacted in August 1974 and which in Massachusetts has been coupled with MHFA developments) still has not been tested as a viable incentive for promoting new development. Federal coinsurance or some other means of assuring adequate financing is required before development to meet lower-income family housing needs can continue.

The greatest effectiveness of new developments will lie in promoting income-mixing and knitting together the ravelled urban fabric, filling vacant or cleared land in ways that contribute to overall neighborhood confidence. As yet, how to do this surely without causing all to seek more subsidies is not fully understood.

Federally-assisted code enforcement (FACE), known in Boston as the Community Improvement Program, has had mixed success. The experience in areas with continuing effective housing demand (e.g., Jamaica Plain) suggests that reasonable code enforcement in itself can be a sufficient impetus to property improvement in such areas and subsidized loans were largely unnecessary. (The attractions of sec. 312 3 percent home loans were offset by aversion to the

13. Income mixing to include market rate tenants is probably a vital factor in the comparative success of MHFA developments. See MHFA Social Audit Summary, *All in Together; A Report on Income-Mixing in Multi-Family Housing,* March 1974.

accompanying red tape and to dealing with "City Hall.") On the other hand, where the housing demand was weakening, code enforcement assisted through subsidized loans was not enough to restore investor confidence and even subsidized outlays were judged by many owners as irrecoverable at resale.

In such weakening areas, the loss of neighborhood confidence often arises from conditions in absentee-owned structures scattered within the neighborhood. Typically four out of five structures (triple deckers or whatever) are occupied by resident owners, and ownership of the fifth has fallen to outsiders through inheritance, or remained tied to an owner who moved out, but did not sell. In other cases, the fifth structure has become part of a large-scale investor's inventory. In any case, maintenance, conditions, and sometimes class of tenants in the fifth structure affect the abutters adversely. The fifth structure is usually the entry point of factors that undermine neighborhood confidence. In the future, programs to boost such confidence, and in particular, to counter influences from the fifth structure will be most critical to preserving the city's existing housing.

Adequate residential credit at affordable terms has been a perennial problem in Boston since the early 1960s when the Boston Banks Urban Renewal Group (BBURG) was initially created to assure a private flow of credit for all "bankable" loan applications originating in federally-assisted program areas. In the late 1960s Mayor White formalized this commitment into an assigned risk pool for mortgages, and lender participation grew substantially under the recently extended FHA 100 percent mortgage insurance.

BBURG was brought to an abrupt halt in 1971 after four years of formal operation by a U.S. Senate subcommittee's hearings (Senator Hart) into widespread charges of racial blockbusting, irregularities in FHA inspections, bank red-lining, etc. The sudden availability of low down payment, fully-insured mortgages radically affected housing dynamics within the closely circumscribed BBURG lending area. Although the lenders were not hurt financially—some even rewrote older 4 to 5 percent mortgages as fully insured 6½ to 7 percent mortgages—the banks have acted deeply wounded by the unfavorable publicity, and have since appeared extremely unsure and cautious about continuing urban lending. However, investors, who already have real estate holdings as collateral, have continued to obtain credit from elsewhere, enabling them to take over structures that were previously occupied by resident owners. Recent attempts to alter lending practices through legislated mortgage disclosure, anti-redlining statutes, etc., appear to assert that home mortgage credit is a neighborhood right of the depositors, leading to polarization on this issue.[14] In fact, the issue is how to make more bankable loans to resident owners. This involves both bolstering effective market demand in some neighborhoods, as well as modifying the lenders' perception of bankable loan applications.

The foremost cause of spreading blight appears to be the inability of households to meet the rising costs of adequate housing, and where too many such households with inadequate income become clustered, unscrupulous absentee owners come to dominate, and the area develops a stigma which adversely affects willingness to maintain housing and future housing demand. Ideally, ways to prevent such clustering and exploitation should be devised to prevent blight.

Conventional housing theory holds that housing ages and filters downward in quality, while people filter upwards. Urban renewal was based on this theory and called for new structures to replace the old. But some FHA housing already appears very blighted, and much of the old housing that was not demolished has been recycled by market demand into good condition. Clearly housing age or conditions per se do not determine the future dynamics of neighborhoods: there are more subtle forces determining who are the replacement buyers and the new residents, and shaping their impact of housing demand on the maintenance of the stock. Neighborhoods in which some representatives of the middle class remain appear to be much less vulnerable to blight and disinvestment, and furthermore, class heterogeneity often encourages a continuous effective housing demand, whereas neighborhoods unaccepting of outsiders have difficulty replenishing themselves with future residents who can afford to maintain the housing as the current ones move or pass on. These neighborhoods then suddenly find themselves without enough replacement resident owner-buyers and tenants, and then the influence of less scrupulous absentee-owners comes to dominate.

Guidelines for the Future

Based on the lessons of the past fifteen years and the problems endemic to many of Boston's submarkets, several guidelines can be identified to which a housing policy should conform:

1. Public resources must be invested in ways which build on market strengths and accommodate market weaknesses; their objective must be to increase private sector confidence and investment of resources rather than simply to underwrite costs.

2. Forms of housing assistance—cash payments, credit or technical assistance—should stress aid to the household rather than to

14. The related issues are explored more fully in Chapter 4, pages 69-82.

the shelter itself, increasing freedom of choice, access to new forms of ownership, and improvement of skills.

3. Subsidies must be carefully designed and administered to promote general neighborhood confidence and continuing conventional maintenance rather than dependence on more subsidies. If nonrecipients become jealous of beneficiaries, or wait for "their turn" at a subsidy that may never extend to all qualified applicants (instead of continuing to maintain their structures), then the subsidy is counterproductive. General and lasting public benefits to those other than the immediate recipients must be evident to justify limited housing subsidies.

4. Policies affecting housing cash flow—code enforcement, property tax assessment and collection, and rent control—must emphasize and provide incentives for preservation of the dwelling structure.

5. Concern must be citywide, rather than selective, concentrating on a few neighborhoods which have reached a highly deteriorated state. Nevertheless, strategies must be tailored to the characteristics of each market area, as well as address themselves to problems shared by most housing suppliers and consumers.

6. Given limited city resources without large-scale federal subsidies, a high priority must be placed on preserving neighborhood confidence. Stabilization and preservation efforts require only a fraction of the resources required for new construction or for futile efforts to prematurely restore confidence in areas of serious deterioration. Preventive care today would obviate the formidable efforts otherwise required in the future to reverse decline and demolish and replace existing housing.

MAINTAINING NEIGHBORHOOD CONFIDENCE

The underlying theme of the previous sections has been that the confidence of any neighborhood in its future is the decisive factor shaping housing dynamics. While simple to state, the presence or absence of such confidence is extraordinarily difficult to measure or index, since it consists of the aggregate perceptions of residents, owners, brokers, lenders, and public officials, as well as the public at large.[15] At the same time, it is important to gauge accurately, since housing policy must be tailored to the confidence level if it is to be effective.

15. Individual perceptions often vary. Some take their cues from the quality and condition of the stock; others from the class of in-migrating residents, or the neighborhood's location. What counts is the aggregate of all these separate perceptions.

The simplest indicator or proxy for confidence which can be used by planners and policymakers is the ratio between active buyers and sellers. Where this ratio increases greater than one, confidence waxes and the probability of speculation enters; and where it declines below one, confidence wanes and the likelihood of disinvestment becomes more real. Underlying all the countless conscious decisions affecting housing is always the basic question—are there enough willing buyers to match sellers who want to sell, or enough tenants to fill vacancies that are opening up?[16]

City strategies then should promote and maintain neighborhood confidence, and prevent the extremes of too many desiring to be in certain areas (like the South End) and too few in others (like Arbutus-Lucerne near Franklin Field). Ideally, the goal of a housing policy should be to enable demand to match supply in the marketplace with a minimum of government intervention. If means could be found, excess demand for particular neighborhoods—on the part of students or a reentrant class of young professionals, for example— should be channeled to neighborhoods with inadequate demand.

Viewed in this new light, traditional housing tools remain important, but they must be administered with greater discretion. A neighborhood's loss of confidence may derive from low resident incomes, or from speculative or exploitive actions on the part of some of the housing suppliers. In the former case, employment programs, income transfers, subsidies or housing assistance may be appropriate; in the latter, code enforcement and rent control can be effective if responsively administered—but it is important neither to subsidize the exploiters nor to cite the low-income owners for code violations that will only exacerbate their financial plight without improving housing conditions. Traditional tools such as these must be employed with a heightened awareness of how their application affects neighborhood confidence.

HOUSING STRATEGIES TAILORED TO NEIGHBORHOOD DYNAMICS

Each of the cells in the neighborhood classification framework (shown as a matrix in fig. 3-9), reflects the current condition and demand situation of a portion of Boston's housing. Over time neighbors tend to shift into different cells when not countered by proper maintenance and upgrading, "pushing housing downward"—that is, the physical condition of the housing deteriorates so that it needs

16. This ratio is not readily available, but interviews with brokers, residents, lenders, and investors will provide it.

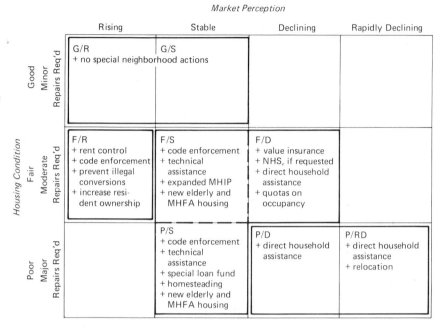

Figure 3-9. Assistance Strategies for Neighborhood Housing Revitalization

greater repairs. More complex forces shape housing demand, the ratios between buyers and sellers, which effectively "moves" neighborhoods to the left or right in the matrix. These factors include location, housing style and quality, as well as actual physical and social conditions.

Amenities such as open space, and specialized land uses such as educational and medical institutions, can bolster housing demand, perhaps even attract new, more affluent people into a neighborhood —in effect "recycling" the neighborhood. Policymakers control or can influence the location of these uses and amenities. The demographic characteristics of present occupants and possible future occupants also shape housing demand, particularly when students or minorities enter the picture. Thus, an influx of students into a neighborhood of families with children can lead to rising prices (or a shift to the left in the matrix), while fear of racial change in a previously all-white neighborhood may reduce the number of qualified traditional buyers (shift to the right), or suddenly bring in new buyers, absentees or non-whites. Housing market behavior can thus become very erratic and uncertain, causing both reduced and inflated sales prices and increased rents. An understanding of these dynamics aids in the identification of appropriate interventions to improve housing conditions and to shift as much housing stock as possible into a stable market state, requiring only moderate repairs (F/S) or better. This entails reducing the attractiveness of some areas while enhancing others.

To achieve the goal of housing restoration thus requires (1) that dwellers have adequate incomes to afford decent housing, and (2) that qualified buyers balance willing sellers in each neighborhood. These conditions must be met if private capital, including resources available to resident owners, is to be tapped or brought into play in housing fix-up. Otherwise only public resources will be used, and they are clearly insufficient. Since the $300 million required to fix up Boston's housing (let alone the much higher costs of replacing abandoned units) is clearly beyond the fiscal capacity of the city, policy must be used to complement and provide leverage over the private incentives for making housing repairs.

Before discussing specific neighborhood strategies in detail, several points must be stressed. The neighborhood strategies proposed are formulated within a citywide housing policy context. The elements of citywide policy include adequate credit; equity in, and reduction of, the burden of property taxation; reorientation of city agencies (such as code enforcement) toward housing consumer services; and reorganization of city agencies to improve the delivery of housing services. These are all discussed in the next chapter.

A housing restoration program must also distinguish between problems which can be resolved by a single injection of public resources as contrasted with problems that will require more sustained public support like income maintenance or transfer payments. In areas where household income was adequate to guarantee routine upkeep, one-shot fix-up funds like Section 312 and 115 loans and grants coupled with areawide code enforcement were effective in returning areas to good condition. But in some lower income areas, these tactics only temporarily improved housing because inadequate cash flow is again leading to deferred maintenance.

Public policy must be designed to increase the attractiveness of each area and the confidence in its future, not simply to underwrite fix-up costs. Without replacement owners to fill the vacancies of those who move away through natural turnover, any neighborhood quickly becomes blighted.

The remedial strategies discussed below are intended to sustain and renew market confidence and to curb the expansion of blight. The proposed strategies for stable and rising markets are aimed at improving the existing stock and will seem familiar; the strategies for declining areas are more novel approaches aimed at supporting and assisting households directly. Resource transfers to needy residents are required to ensure that the inability to pay for adequate housing does not cause neighborhood decline wherever poor families live. The costs of such income assistance are large but inescapable. They are a direct consequence of our rising general standard of living.

The newly emerging housing policy for the city adds the perception of neighborhood dynamics to housing condition data to arrive at newly orchestrated housing tools. Figure 3-9 summarizes the city's revitalization strategies, and figure 3-10 displays the associated public expenditures. Administrative costs have not been computed and the program estimates contain no allowance for inflation. The purpose of these estimates is simply to convey the orders of magnitude involved in eliminating substandard housing in various market contexts.

Remedial Strategies for Stable Markets

Stable areas where housing is in good condition (G/S) do not require special neighborhood housing actions by the city beyond appropriate routine public improvements, city services, and equitable shares of the citywide strategies discussed in Chapter 4.

Technical assistance, code enforcement, and property tax incentives linked to repairs will maintain stability and improve conditions in stable areas needing moderate fix-up (F/S).

The original intent of the federally-assisted code enforcement program—to combine special fix-up incentives with areawide code enforcement and public improvements—remains valid. Unfortunately, federal 3 percent loans were always uncertain and encumbered by red tape; the code standards have been raised beyond limits that many tenants and owners can afford—but a carrot-and-stick approach focused on marginal neighborhoods remains an appropriate approach. In these areas the city can encourage improvements through services-oriented code enforcement[17] coupled with technical support such as rehabilitation counseling to owners who request it. The code enforcement costs could be met from the regular city budget, but technical assistance would be a new expense. For

---

17. Reorganized and reoriented code enforcement is recommended. Inspectors should focus on these stable and rising areas and provide brief write-ups of remedial work required instead of adopting a punitive stance and simply citing a list of violations. Systematic code inspections in declining areas can achieve little until more fundamental family income problems are addressed. The section of Chapter 4, subtitled "creating a Service Orientation in City Regulatory Departments" (pages 88-92), discusses proposed changes in codes administration to achieve the desired results.

Figure 3-10.   Estimated Public Expenditures Associated with Neighborhood Assistance Strategies, 1975-1985

Area[1]	# Units	Percent	Annual Technical Assistance	Annual Fix-Up Grants	Special Loan Fund	Annual Direct Assistance	Relocation	Demolition
F/S	56,400	23%	$225,600 ($4/d.u.)	$282,000 ($5/d.u.)				
P/S	22,000	9%	220,000 ($10/d.u.)	220,000 ($10/d.u.)	$2,200,000 ($100/d.u.)			
F/D	12,800	6%				$9,216,000 ($720/hh)		
P/D	17,300	8%				18,684,000 ($1,080/hh)		
P/RD	1,600	1%				1,728,000 ($1,080/hh)	$480,000 ($300/hh)	
Annual Totals All Areas		47%	$445,600[2]	$502,000[2]	$2,200,000	$29,628,000	$480,000	
Decade Totals All Areas	110,036		$4,456,000[2]	$5,020,000[2]	$11,000,000[3]	$296,280,000[4]	$480,000[5]	2,227,000[6]

1. Areas other than those listed have no special public costs.
2. Fix-up is complete at the close of the decade, requiring no additional expenditures.
3. This revolving loan fund is repayable by borrowers or recoverable through Lens.
4. These costs would continue as long as households continue to qualify.
5. Once relocation is complete, no further expenditures in this category are needed.
6. Demolitions would be scheduled as buildings are vacated in declining areas.

the roughly 55,000 units in F/S areas, these additional public expenditures are estimated to run to $2.2 million, or $220,000 per year for ten years, (averaging out to $4 per unit per year).[18]

The technical assistance costs could be financed through a combination of public and private funds. Depending on their financial standing, some recipients of these services could be asked to repay their costs, particularly if they could reimburse them through an amortizing loan. Repair costs themselves could usually be borne by owners who can draw on their own rainy day savings ("mattress money") or take out short-term home improvement loans.[19]

During 1975 the city of Boston committed federal community development block grants towards expanding the Housing Improvement Program (HIP) into a program of technical assistance and 20 percent direct cash rebates to resident owners of 1-6 unit structures who brought their buildings into code compliance.[20] The HIP also granted these owners immunity from property tax reassessment for these repairs. Eight months after its official announcement, over 8,000 owners are involved in upgrading their structures under this program, nearly one in ten of those eligible, and an evaluation on the types of participating owners, repairs, average expenses, and sources of financing is expected in the winter of 1976. It is already clear that most owners are doing much of the work themselves or arranging their own contractors, and largely using "mattress money," viewing the HIP as an opportunity. At present, all absentee-owned structures are ineligible, and many lower-income households are financially unable to participate. In the future, this promising pro-

18. This estimate draws on experiences in a wide variety of private fix-up programs from Rochester, N.Y., Pittsburgh, Pa., and Cambridge, Mass. We have made the following assumptions to illustrate the order of magnitude of public expenditures to fix-up all F/S areas. (1) Technical assistance is estimated at $200 per dwelling unit, or an average of $500 per structure; (2) Only one out of every five houses utilizes technical assistance; (3) There are about 55,000 units in F/S areas; (4) Technical assistance in any particular area can be spread over four years, and technical assistance throughout all F/S areas of the city will be phased over ten years.

Thus, for the 55,000 units in F/S areas, technical assistance averages $40 per unit (i.e., $200 x 1/5) and requires a total outlay of $2.2 million or $220,000 per year if the entire city wide program is phased over ten years. This is comparable to costs in Pittsburgh, Cambridge, Springfield (Mass.), and Rochester (N.Y.), for assistance in obtaining loans and arranging for proper fix-up, or alternatively, guidance in providing "sweat" equity.

19. Chapter 864 of the Massachusetts Legislature, Acts of 1974 was enacted to encourage greater urban lending and to authorize public reimbursements for technical assistance. This bill was drafted with the intent of promoting home improvements in stable areas requiring moderate repairs (see Chapter 4), p. 80.

20. See R. Goetze, "Housing Rehab is a Winner in Boston," in *Planning*, January 1976, pp. 4-5, American Society of Planning Officials.

gram should be modified and become part of a comprehensive strategy to improve all residential structures in a neighborhood rather than just those of resident owners who are committed to improving their housing. This is likely to involve sanctions like code enforcement or rent reductions upon owners who deliberately undermaintain[21] and extending fix-up incentives to absentee-owners of good standing. In special cases deeper financial assistance may promote fix-up, but this should be employed sparingly and only in instances where aiding a particular structure can decisively spur other owners to invest on their own, rather than cause them to also demand special assistance. The city is currently designing such a comprehensive approach to housing fix-up. A critical component in this strategy will be code standards that the majority of structures in a neighborhood can meet. Residents can help define such standards, and the city must be ready to use this "stick" on substandard housing suppliers; the various "carrot" incentives alone will prove inadequate to promote fix-up, because many owners will not invest until the "blighters" are dealt with.

Such fix-up incentives should be offered only during the first two years of systematic code enforcement in any area (as a device for initiating the fix-up process). For the 56,400 units in F/S areas, these fix-up incentives are estimated to require $2.82 million in public expenditures to complete fix-up of this vital one-quarter of the city stock—a good investment as compared with its potential market value. This would require about $282,000 annually if the city schedules the program for the appropriate F/S areas over ten years.[22] If the program were extended citywide, fix-up reimburse-

---

21. While such owners are few, their impact is often devastating to neighborhood confidence. These owners often also are delinquent in their taxes, are responsible for a disproportionate share of Housing Court cases, etc.

22. Costs are estimated as follows: assuming eligible areas were targeted, (similar to those meeting criteria of federally-assisted code enforcement (FACE) program areas), overall costs could be controlled by matching area sizes to federal resources such as might become available under community development revenue sharing. Assuming further that grants average $500 per unit, that only the "early adopters" in the first two years in any designated areas utilize them, that only one-fifth of all eligible recipients are early adopters, and that half the dwellings are eligible due to resident ownership, a maximum of one out of ten units in F/S areas would receive compensation and maximum costs would reach $2,820,000 (or $500 x 1/10 x 56,400 units). While such a program would be targeted for F/S areas, its benefits should still be available during the same time period to *all* resident owners in the city who remove code violations, regardless of their income. (This would shift costs forward, increasing them initially, but reducing them in later years.)

ments would still average about $500 per unit, but citywide implementation would dilute the grant program's effectiveness. The program's capacity to encourage fix-up, instead of simply compensating for routine maintenance, lies in being implemented systematically on an *area-by-area* basis and making the grants only during a two-year period to spur rapid, concentrated improvements, "to get the ball rolling."

Stable areas needing major repairs (P/S) require the addition of a special loan fund to supplement technical assistance and code enforcement as part of a comprehensive fix-up program. Some owners in such neighborhoods have savings, but not all can afford the costs of extensive fix-up. During the 1960s, the federally-assisted 312-115 loan and grant program was designed to meet the needs of such owners. In Pittsburgh a cost-effective, flexible way of meeting these requirements has been developed by creating a special loan fund under the joint control of community and lending institution representatives.[23] Managers of this loan fund can cosign or subsidize the interest for conventional home improvement loans, as well as make direct loans. When one case in four, the "unbankable" case, was assisted through this special loan fund, conventional lenders accepted the less needy three out of four cases and provided them with direct loans.

A similar Neighborhood Housing Services (NHS) program was initiated in Boston during the summer of 1974. Experience in other cities with NHS suggests that such a fund can start with as little as $100 per dwelling unit in the area at the outset. The fund should be built up to $500 per dwelling and can sustain itself at that level through re-payments. For the 22,000 dwellings in P/S areas, this estimate would require $2.2 million at the beginning and an eventual $11 million. These are not public costs, however, because they are repaid to the loan fund by property owners either as amortizing loans over a five- to ten-year period or as lump sums upon eventual sales of the fixed-up properties. The only nonrecoverable expenses are (1) differences between interest earned by the fund and market rates, (2) any losses or direct subsidies, and (3) administrative costs.

The cost of technical assistance and incentives for fix-up must also be reckoned as public expenditures in P/S areas. More in-depth technical assistance is likely to be needed by a larger fraction of the owners in P/S than in F/S areas, where less fix-up is needed. It is

23. See page 92, and footnote #30, where Neighborhood Housing Services of Pittsburgh is discussed in greater detail.

estimated that the 22,000 units will require $2.2 million in technical assistance and $2.2 million in cash rebates along with the $11 million loan fund to upgrade the P/S areas over ten years, or $220,000 annually.[24]

The role of *new construction* in meeting Boston's housing needs is undergoing a critical reappraisal. During the 1960s it was taken for granted that new construction was a solution to urban blight; and a rapid pace of development was maintained, increasingly through use of subsidies. However, both low- and moderate-income housing needs, as well as housing abandonment have perceptibly increased since the early 1960s, casting doubt in some minds on the efficacy of new construction in improving residential neighborhoods.

In the longer run, however, new development remains an important component of Boston's housing programs. For the next decade, targets have been set for 20,000 units of new construction based on the identified continuing strong housing demand and on special needs such as the elderly. New development is an important tool, not only in providing jobs, but in promoting neighborhood stability in all areas where demand holds up. Locating such housing in weak demand areas, however, is not appropriate because developments will prove unable to attract market rate tenants vital for income-mixing.

Costs for new development are not included in public expenditures shown in figure 3-10 because it is not intrinsically required for preserving Boston's housing. Current cost estimates approach $40,000 per family unit, or require a Section 8 subsidy of over $3,500 per household per annum!

Residential development should be planned on the income-mixing principles governing MHFA developments and a target of 12,000 units has been set, 50 percent for middle- and upper-income occupancy, and the balance for low- and moderate-income households. Subsidies like the federal section 8-leased housing program should be coordinated into conventionally-financed developments in locations where such new development promotes neighborhood strength. The safeguard of sound development lies in exempting a significant

24. Costs are estimated as follows: Assuming an average technical assistance cost of $300 per unit, and utilization by an average of one of three owners, one-third of the 22,000 units in P/S areas will need assistance. At $300 per unit, this requires an outlay of $2,200,000 or $220,000 per year if phased over ten years. (Any particular area should be completed in 3-4 years, however, for visible impact to make all residents conscious of the revitalization effort.) Bonuses for fix-up, like those outlined above for F/S areas, would average $500 per unit. If one-fifth the units in P/S areas needed them, total costs would be 22,000 x 1/5 x $500, or $2,200,000 spread over a ten-year period. Implemented area by area, staged over ten years, bonuses would cost around $220,000 per year.

fraction of the units in each development permanently from subsidized occupancy, thereby forcing developers to evaluate the demand before they embark on construction. One hundred percent subsidized demand will simply permit repetition or exacerbation of the costly mistakes that already haunt recently produced subsidized housing.

An important part of Boston's housing program is directed towards the elderly, because of the special housing needs of this population group, and because the elderly comprise a significant portion of the city's homeowners. Many of these needs may best be served through new housing production.

Elderly citizens have special housing problems which should be met, and the quantitative dimensions are significant. A target of building 8,000 units of elderly housing has been set—5,000 of this as public housing, and 3,000 to be built through other subsidized housing programs such as the federal 236 program or the MHFA. The purpose of such a target is twofold: first, to provide better housing for the elderly; and second, to benefit the nonelderly population as the large units which many small elderly households currently rent or own come on the market.

In addition, all encouragement should be given to those seeking to experiment with such new uses of the existing housing stock which would benefit the elderly, such as the creation of "mother-in-law" apartments, or the conversion of small hotels or large houses into congregate housing facilities.

Homesteading has a vastly overrated potential, particularly as a device for stabilizing declining areas. In areas where demand and prices have stabilized, however, tax foreclosed and delinquent properties are suitable for conveyance to new resident owners who can meet a downpayment requirement and are able to devise their own approaches to fixing them up. Homesteaders will need the technical assistance and fix-up tax incentives described above, but they will need much larger amounts of housing credits, up to $10–12,000 per unit, to make the extensive improvements needed in these much more seriously deteriorated and usually unoccupied properties. If this level of private credit is not available, homesteading will fail. These properties should not be assigned high priority for the allocation of scarce public resources, however, since each dwelling unit requires so many dollars. Rather, rapid removal of abandoned structures in areas of declining demand should be considered because their presence encourages such disinvestment. Their removal, coupled with leasing the cleared sites as gardens, can go a long way to stabilize the markets.

Homesteading is appropriate mainly where a market has already "bottomed-out" and is not about to decline further. In declining areas where additional abandonment is anticipated, rational owners would not continue maintaining, let alone investing heavily, in rehabilitation of their properties, because these investments could not be recovered. Any homesteader in such cases would become locked into this property, having only "negative equity" to show for his renovation efforts.

Demolition. Neighborhood revitalization also requires dealing rapidly with the few sorely deteriorated structures that have effectively been abandoned by their owners. In the past such structures were often boarded up, intended for future rehabilitation, but experience has shown that few were ever successfully restored. Their blighting presence often discouraged abutters from further maintenance and upkeep, as well as warned appraisers and new buyers that supply exceeded demand, so these structures did much more harm than their potential value as future housing resources could ever offset. As yet, there is no practical, inexpensive way to "moth ball" such structures for future use after effective housing demand in the area is restored—and their very presence prevents the restoration of demand. In the interim, these structures drain public resources. Some catch fire, others function as havens for crime or pose hazards for curious children. Demolition of unwanted structures has become an important tool in revitalizing neighborhoods. Many outsiders are stunned that the net benefits of demolition far exceed "trying to restore a scarce housing resource," but this merely stresses how important understanding the nature of the particular market is to neighborhood fix-up.

Demolition costs, roughly $1,000 per unit or $2,227,000, were already indicated in the citywide condition survey. Most demolitions would be required in the P/D and P/RD neighborhoods, but it is especially critical to demolish abandoned structures in stable areas if no one will restore them to the stock without subsidies.

In Boston, over $1 million of community development revenues are being devoted to such a rapid demolition program which results in cleared, loamed over lots, often leased to abutters to plant a garden or the like while title problems are resolved. The city will soon have eliminated the backlog of abandoned structures.

Remedial Strategies for Rising Markets

City administrators should identify the excessively strong market (G/R) neighborhoods with good housing and maintain an effective regulatory posture towards them to discourage undue rent increases and illegal conversions. Speculative rent increases should not be necessary since the housing stock in these areas is basically in good repair and outlays are only rarely needed to correct deficiencies or to modernize. However, in such areas speculatively inclined owners are tempted to reap the gains of rising market values without any improvements in services. Proper code enforcement and publicizing property tax reassessments on those who sharply inflate rents can help encourage responsible ownership. In cities like Boston, with a Rent Control Administration, many of the applications for rent increases come from G/R areas. Financial sophistication on the part of municipal regulatory agencies is required to allow increases where they are due without fueling further inflation of housing prices throughout such areas.

When speculation does get out of hand, tenant-landlord polarization increases, and formerly sound housing can erode surprisingly rapidly. When such collapse of the housing market occurs the shrewdest owners have usually already taken their windfall gains elsewhere and sold their properties to less experienced amateurs or newcomers.[25]

Appropriate neighborhood strategies for F/R areas include special emphasis on code enforcement, assessing and rent control functions (where present), monitoring illegal conversions, and widening ownership options. Except for extending ownership forms, these policies encompass municipal land use powers and should be provided by the city's appropriate regulatory agencies. In F/R neighborhoods conditions are only fair while the market is rising and this calls for careful public intervention to protect the interest of less affluent residents in the face of the appreciating market.

Fixing up housing in rising market areas poses a dilemma. Countervailing social forces may be present. Existing tenants, often on fixed incomes, may seek improvements but be unable to meet the rent increases required to pay for them. Landlords may be willing to make the improvements but will want to raise rents accordingly, especially when they know they can attract a new, more affluent tenant who can afford the higher price. This process must be monitored to ensure that landlords do not try to capitalize on the rising market by asking for rent increases which are not justified by improvements. Absentee owners frequently have more speculative interests and therefore require close monitoring to prevent illegal

25. The Boston Redevelopment Authority is currently studying these dynamics under the direction of the author in a recently initiated investigation tentatively titled "Study of Multi-Family Investor-Owned Properties."

conversions. But public regulation does not solve the problem of tenants without the means to pay for housing fix-up. In the long run, the rights of such residents to remain as tenants in rising markets are difficult to safeguard without increasing the tenants' ability to remain through some direct subsidy to those households. Only by opening options of ownership like condominiums or cooperatives to tenants in multi-unit structures can they be protected from being displaced by more affluent households.

Wherever repairs are required amidst a strong market demand, the dilemma is to clarify the rights of tenants with limited incomes to remain. Should they be allowed to live in substandard dwellings? If not, how much of the improvement costs should be passed on in increased rents? If there were either public subsidies to pay for the fix-up (like low-interest loans) or direct rental assistance to tenants (through Sec. 8 leased housing), these could be granted to owners upon the conditions that they make the improvements and continue to serve the existing tenants. But at present neither subsidy nor direct assistance is generally available and conditions involving income limitations tend to develop into an administrative nightmare even when such assistance programs are operative.

Creating condominium options for present tenants offers more promise. This would enable them to share in the rising market instead of being displaced by it. As owners, they could benefit from increasing equity based on rising markets. Additional benefits of condominium ownership include income tax deductions for mortgage interest and property tax payments the impact of which depend on the owner's tax bracket. With the current rapidly-increasing pace of inflation, many more households will be in the tax brackets where cooperative or condominium ownership could reduce their net housing expenses while providing them with equity. These forms of tenure are already being adopted for modest-income households under special housing programs in Cambridge.[26] Similar adaptations could be made in certain Boston rising market neighborhoods if good counseling and technical assistance were made available. At this stage a pilot effort by a community based nonprofit institution would be an appropriate test of this proposed approach.

Extending these forms of tenure does not entail public program expenditures, but requires altering housing credit policies of con-

26. Work Equity and Homeowners Rehab, Inc., 678 Massachusetts Ave. Cambridge, Mass., has pioneered this process locally, enabling lower income families to become condominium owners in four-story, frame, row housing on Broadway at favorable prices in strong market areas. The city of Cambridge is giving this organization support under community development revenue sharing to continue and expand this program.

servative lenders, and devising master deeds applicable to triple deckers or row houses. Individual proposals for moderate-income condominiums are already in the discussion stage and the next steps are analysis and dissemination of the possibilities. In the long run, the city stands to gain from such conversions, both through neighborhood maintenance which typically accompanies resident ownership (and which preserves a sound tax base), and possibly through some increased tax yield. However, care should be taken in applying tax policy to these forms of ownership because sharply increased assessments (due to condominium conversions or rising values) can easily drive out residents with limited incomes.

Remedial Strategies for Declining Areas

The strategies for assisting areas that are declining differ radically from those appropriate for sound and rising market areas because the challenge is to appreciably increase housing demand. Homeowners, if they are concerned about the condition of their property, feel that forces they cannot fight are causing the decline: curtailed availability of lending and insurance, fear of lower rental incomes from new residents, racial change; and as the self-fulfilling trend continues, visible deterioration, accumulating debris and trash. Those who see housing primarily as an investment—both absentee property owners and banks—are inclined to overreact at the early stages of decline. Fearing deteriorating property values, they begin to disinvest, curtail maintenance, and extract what they still can out of their properties.

Under these circumstances, a very unstable situation results, changing long-term resident owners into sellers. Statistics in Boston indicate that annual owner turnover is normally between 4 and 8%, meaning that among a thousand structures perhaps 50 seek a buyer annually. As long as there are over 50 willing and qualified buyers the neighborhood remains stable, but if only 40 buyers show up, the other 950 owners become more inclined to disinvest unless active neighborhood promotion begins. Suddenly, there are many more sellers than buyers. Some owners may panic, willing to sell now rather than face the uncertainty of obtaining less later on. Other owners, hearing of price declines may become frightened and also start dumping their property for whatever price, however low, it can bring. As people overreact, the bottom falls out of the market. Ironically, housing conditions may be fairly good before this process begins and racial change may in fact not occur, but as more prosperous and informed households depart, less responsive absentee owners replace them. New interest groups such as brokers (who exploit residents' fears and who may engage in FHA speculation) and low-income tenant advocates (who adopt a very aggressive posture against all owners in attempts to secure improved housing) appear in the neighborhood. Landlords and tenants become polarized, one group holding the other solely responsible for deteriorating housing conditions. Each may develop unrealistic expectations about the other's financial resources and ability to pay for housing improvements. This process plays itself out to housing abandonment in some all-white neighborhoods where there is no effective housing demand acceptable to the residents.

The lack of housing demand acceptable to the current residents is a key factor in the decline of such neighborhoods. Beyond this the uncertainty about the future fosters disinvestment: What will this neighborhood be like? Will white speculators take over? Will "white trash" or blacks move in? Will my wife and children be able to walk the streets? Will my property be firebombed? Such worries are magnified by rumor and sensationalism. Residents who can, leave at all costs. Those who remain are the less sophisticated who are more easily preyed upon.

Any effective fight against decline depends on initiative and promotion from within the neighborhoods. Attempts to save a declining neighborhood solely from the outside generally fail. The attitudes of residents are key variables. Will the most capable local leaders stay and promote the neighborhood, or will they flee? City services and the strategies previously discussed for stable neighborhoods can *prevent* decay only in neighborhoods that have confidence in their own future. Code enforcement, technical assistance, and even special loan funds are useful only when they complement neighborhood self-initiatives. Imposed from outside, or brought in by an insignificant minority of residents, they will be unable to effect housing upgrading.

To make public improvements visible and to promise an improvement in city services are not enough. Rebuilding or replacing existing housing under the programs similar to the federal subsidy programs of the 1960s is not only too cumbersome but tends to undermine neighborhood confidence and to reduce market demand when the subsidized beneficiaries are not seen as meritorious by the existing residents. The recently-curtailed federal housing and urban renewal programs were largely supply-oriented and often provided few benefits for the existing neighborhood residents. They did not reckon with the need of *low-income households* for jobs and more income resources. Too often they rehoused a few while scattering the majority and provoking resident owners to depart.

Direct household assistance to all eligible residents of declining areas should be tried as an alternative to housing production assistance. Direct financial assistance in the form of either housing allowances or income supports coupled with job training and counseling gives priority to helping households, instead of to saving or replacing specific residential structures in declining areas.[27] This approach could open up a wider range of housing choices for all these households than supply-side programs did. With more money in their pockets, the effective housing demand of low-income families would be substantially strengthened. Individually they could elect whether to remain in their present neighborhoods, utilizing their additional resources to obtain improvements on their present dwellings or to move to better neighborhoods, gaining entry with their increased ability to pay for adequate housing.[28] Thus demonstrated consumer preferences for housing will be a better guide to identifying which neighborhoods have a future and which are obsolescing than leaning on the policies of lending institutions or public bureaucracies. Areas where most households choose to remain become stable by definition. The city would then respond by providing the housing improvement programs available to F/S and P/S areas: technical assistance, tax incentives and special loan funds.

Direct household assistance coupled with income maintenance to all eligible households in weak market areas compares favorably to supply side subsidy per unit cost even though it aggregates to substantial public expenditures. In areas where decline is accompanied by the need for major repairs (P/D), substantial assistance averaging about $90 monthly per household residing in the qualifying areas would be required. Such assistance should be tailored to income, family size, and the cost of standard housing (much like the formulas used by HUD in the several housing allowance experiments), and

27. The optimum form of assistance should minimize red tape and maximize increased purchasing power. To prevent inflation, phasing-in must be gradual to allow the local housing submarket to respond constructively to the new purchasing power and to give fix-up contractors time to bring dwellings up to code. Safeguards to prevent occupancy of substandard dwellings at higher rents must be carefully designed to prevent bureaucratic restrictions of consumer choice. One promising way to introduce this assistance that avoids many of the pitfalls would be to grant the assistance to only a fraction of the eligible households participating in any specific market in the first year, much like the draft lottery, or qualifying only certain digits in the household head's social security number. Only after several years would every household receive assistance. Letting qualified households select units and simply canceling further assistance to any dwellings while they fail to meet code standards is probably the simplest effective approach.

28. Preliminary indications from the national housing allowance experiments indicate that when households move, they follow traditional migration routes; i.e., allowances do not foster racial integration. In Springfield, Mass., recipients of housing allowances felt they were definitely improving their housing.

extended to all eligible tenants and owners residing for at least the prior six months in the designated areas. But there should be a minimum of red tape beyond code compliance. (Federal programs, including the housing allowance experiment, tend to develop a myriad of special forms, leases, etc.) The assistance should be allocated to these households for at least five years, whether they remain in the area or move somewhere else, because no matter where they move, their incomes are inadequate to obtain decent housing without the direct assistance.

Annual direct assistance costs for the 17,300 households in P/D areas are estimated at $18.7 million ($1,080 per household per year), which must be financed annually from public funds. This figure does not include start-up or administrative costs. While this sum seems large in the aggregate, it is moderate in comparison to the unit cost outlays for section 8 assistance or new federally subsidized (Section 236) construction in recent years. The value of the Section 236 mortgage interest subsidy alone per unit in Boston averages about $1,200 annually. In addition, property tax concessions, piggybacked federal/state rent supplements, and administrative costs have further escalated public expenditures for such housing subsidy programs. More important, they have failed to restore market confidence in these areas.[29]

Direct household assistance is preferable to subsidies for housing construction and rehabilitation in declining areas because it deals more directly with a key factor in declining housing demand: lack of adequate income to pay for needed housing maintenance.[30]

Relocation should be added to direct assistance in areas where poor conditions and rapid decline compound (particularly in P/RD, because it is likely that most households will elect to move.) Relocation costs for the 1,600 households in P/F areas would be $480,000

29. Currently 58 percent of Boston's households are eligible for federally subsidized housing while there are only enough assisted units to serve one in ten. Section 8-type construction and rehabilitation programs (with costs approaching $40,000 per unit) to meet the needs of all eligible households would be far more costly than the direct assistance proposed here. For a more detailed evaluation of recent Section 221(d)(3) and 236 construction in Boston, see the Boston Redevelopment Authority/Boston Urban Observatory joint study, *Subsidized Multi-Family Rental Housing in the Boston Metropolitan Area: Analysis and Prognosis* (October 1973).

30. It is very difficult to earn a fair return on any housing renting for less than $135/month ($110 plus $25 monthly for heat) in the city of Boston in 1973. But $135/month represents one-quarter of a $6,480 annual income. Many households with substantially lower incomes are attempting to pay this or even greater amounts, but they often have difficulty meeting the rent. Rent delinquencies and skip-outs are a prime cause of blight and neighborhood deterioration. See Michael Stegman, *Housing Investment in the Inner-City: the Dynamics of Decline*, M.I.T. Press, Cambridge, 1971.

($300 per household), a one-time public expense. The precedent for such relocation assistance already exists for households caught in the path of highway construction and urban renewal. Acquisition, clearance or renewal subsidies for these P/RD areas are explicitly not part of the fix-up strategy, but land would become available for redevelopment.

Annual direct assistance costs for the 1,600 households currently in P/RD areas are estimated at $1.73 million (at $1,080 per household per year) from public funds.

Areas where housing conditions are still fair in spite of a declining market demand (F/D) pose dilemmas for planners and policymakers because physical conditions are better than in P/S, P/D, and P/RD areas, fostering the illusion that much less costly supply-side public interventions would be effective for improving housing. Nevertheless, past experience in Boston suggests that once residents believe an area is declining, public improvements, loans and grants, and even new subsidized housing construction will be of little lasting impact in altering these beliefs unless neighborhood promotion can strengthen demand and confidence. While substantial income assistance in declining areas may even accelerate the departure of households in some areas, it is likely to be more effective in aiding households than past strategies because it offers them more choice.

The cost gap in F/D areas is likely to be smaller than in areas where housing requires major repairs, and the extended assistance averages $60 monthly per household (rather than $90). This will require annual public expenditure of some $9.2 million for the 12,800 dwellings in F/D areas ($720 per unit annually).

Continuing credit, value insurance and quotas to control socioeconomic mix are potential tools for improving neighborhood expectations once household assistance is extended to households in declining areas. These tactics are as important to the control of dynamics in currently stable areas as for areas already perceived as declining. They are proposed here merely as policy concepts which require further refinement.

Credit.[31] The regular availability of credit is a major factor in neighborhood preservation. For most owners, the equity in their house is sizable and important. When potential replacement buyers find credit difficult to obtain in a particular neighborhood, they take it as a warning that, were they to buy, they would find resale difficult in the future—and they then buy elsewhere. But current owners also notice this, often begin to disinvest, and some decide

31. Chapter 4 examines this issue in greater detail (see pp. 69-82).

to sell "while they can," leading to a glut of offerings for sale. While there are other causes of weak demand, lack of steady and readily available credit critically affects all housing.

Disintermediation—the periodic massive withdrawal of savings deposits—has nationally stressed the mortgage credit system to its limits, but "red-lining"—discouraging all inner-city loan applications—appears to compound the problem of maintaining a steady availability of credit in "mature urban neighborhoods." As yet, these intertwined factors are not even generally understood. Bankers claim that disintermediation underlies whatever community groups call red-lining.

Past attempts to remedy such problems have backfired. An assigned risk mortgage pool created in the 1960s—the Boston Banks Urban Renewal Group, or BBURG—resulted in a lot of recent HUD-insured foreclosures, as well as many misleading and bitter recriminations between all the interests who tried to make BBURG function. Many are reluctant to grapple with these complex issues again, yet steady availability of adequate credit is one of the most critical elements in neighborhood revitalization. Without it, all special efforts like fix-up incentives will prove futile or useless.

Restoring general access to credit is currently one of the least understood yet most important problems to be resolved in preserving existing neighborhoods. A first step has already been taken through state-mandated disclosure on the part of state-chartered thrift institutions of deposit and lending patterns by zip code. The city is concurrently preparing a data base of normal residential credit by census tracts to use as a benchmark for evaluating the disclosed lending patterns and determining the next steps in restoring adequate residential credit.[32]

Value insurance could insure that housing in fair condition is not caught in a seller's panic. As already pointed out, when economic or racial change threatens an area, too many owners fear losing their equity and put their houses up for sale, thereby depressing sales prices. As prices fall below the unpaid balance of the mortgage, more owners begin to seriously consider abandoning their property. The notion of placing a federally-supported floor under house values has been discussed periodically. Just as fire insurance repays an owner on property loss resulting from fire, similar equity insurance could repay a resident owner (not a lender) his original price plus any appraised improvements if he were unable to recover that value at time of sale (but, would not compensate him for losses due to his own negligence or lack of maintenance). Insuring owners against loss

32. For significantly more detail on these issues, see pp. 78–79.

of equity would put a floor under house values in order to reduce panic sales.

To set up such insurance in a manner preventing fraud is difficult, but since most maintained housing tends to appreciate in value, this program would cost very little if conducted on a broad enough base. If sold on a premium basis, participation by those who feel they do not currently need it would pose a special problem. The city could underwrite such value insurance to assure the future of the tax base. The incentive for the federal or state governments to provide such insurance in addition to existing mortgage insurance is substantial: it would curb both the incentives of existing owners to sell quickly, as well as prevent newer owners from abandoning property because they feared their amortization payments were not building up their equity.

Setting quotas to control socioeconomic mix in the neighborhoods conflicts with free choice and equal opportunity, but the latter goals may currently be unattainable. Although quotas may be too radical for serious consideration as a city strategy to prevent the decline of areas in fair condition, a brief discussion may lead to new insights into the psychological aspects of decline and the discovery of new means to alter trends.[33] The first black households to move into white areas are usually middle income who encourage white resident owners to remain, believing that their presence maintains city services and prevents neighborhood decline. Nevertheless, white households leave and the area usually resegregates into a lower class non-white neighborhood. The notion of a "tipping-point" is now largely seen as an oversimplification. The "tipping-point" notion assumed that racial mix below a certain threshold was tolerable and that the mass exodus of white owners occurs only when the percentage of non-whites exceeds a "tipping-point". Better predictors of neighborhood future than any given percentage of non-whites are the existing residents' perceptions of what future property values and neighborhood quality will be. Attainable and credible quotas on future occupancy could alter these perceptions.

The affluent suburbs have managed to maintain socioeconomic quotas so effectively in their self-interest that most non-white population growth is channeled into resegregating areas. Altering this pattern may require temporary quotas, as affirmative action plans in employment and education have shown. Both the new arrivals and existing residents in a newly integrating neighborhood have a joint interest in the prevention of panic sales and curtailment of lending and city services. Ideally, an ethnically and economically

33. This discussion on trends is explored more thoroughly in Chapter 5.

diverse market would maintain its mix, but market dynamics tend to permit only transitional economic or racial integration. Those who seek to live in areas that remain integrated will have to depend on influencing the process whereby outmigrants are replaced to maintain an optimal mix.

Tactics for insuring continuance of such a distribution are yet to be invented and raise constitutional questions.[34] If such a policy could be devised, it would probably prevent the moving out "before their time" of a host of long-term residents, an exodus which triggers major decline.

COST SUMMARY OF SPECIAL NEIGHBORHOOD STRATEGIES

Conclusions

Figure 3-10 summarizes the estimated annual public costs of the proposed neighborhood strategies and the total public expenditures required to complete fix-up over the decade, allowing the following conclusions to be drawn.

1. Over half the existing housing stock in Boston (53 percent) imposes no additional costs on the municipal budget. Such housing is located in the strong and stable market areas in good condition.

2. An additional third (32 percent) of the stock (areas F/S and P/S) requires annual outlays of under $1 million in technical assistance and fix-up grants over ten years plus a revolving loan fund of $11 million (largely repayable) to complete fix-up of such areas. These are the areas where effective public policy can decisively alter the future by maintaining them instead of allowing blight and abandonment to creep in.

3. Less than one-sixth (15 percent) of the stock (in F/D, P/D, and P/RD areas) is threatened by severe blight, but to meet the needs of the households in these areas alone requires $30 million *annually* in direct assistance and/or income transfer payments. This may look like a staggering sum but it represents an average of less than $1,080 annually (or $90 monthly) per affected household, less than the mortgage interest subsidy alone on each unit of publicly assisted housing and only one third of a household Sec. 8 commitment in

---

34. Ironically, economic exclusionary zoning has been with us for years and constitutional challenges against it are just beginning to be raised. Two recent articles provide an excellent basis for continued discussion of these critical issues. See Daniel Lauber, "Integration Takes More than a Racial Quota," in *Planning* (ASPO Journal), April-May, 1974, and Bruce L. Ackerman, "Integration for Subsidized Housing and the Question of Racial Occupancy Controls," in *Stanford Law Review* 26 (Jan. 1974): 245.

Boston. That blight can be contained for less public outlays is likely to prove illusory and ultimately much more expensive. The above estimates merely close the gap between income and the costs of meeting the housing needs of these households. It is doubtful that this gap can be bridged for much less. Promises to deal with abandonment and severe blight in declining neighborhoods in fair to poor condition through supply side subsidies have consistently proven false. The unit costs of recent supply side interventions are not only higher, but they often fail to provide lasting assistance to households.

4. The $30 million in annual direct assistance gives priority only to households in declining areas. Admittedly, this is programmatically difficult to achieve, but if declining areas can be accurately identified, injecting direct assistance therein would stabilize and assist in preserving as much as possible of Boston's housing stock. If all households eligible on the basis of income (regardless of neighborhood dynamics) were to be served, this annual estimate of expense is likely to be tripled to $90 million.

Caveats

Several comments on the underlying methodology of developing these estimates are in order to forestall criticism of the conclusions.

1. The costs in figure 3-10 are merely illustrative of the orders of magnitude involved. The methodology is spelled out so that better information and analysis can be applied to sharpen the estimates. Obviously, as inflation continues it becomes appropriate to scale the estimates up proportionately. The basic argument remains the same: *it is more cost effective to maintain stable areas than to counter decline once loss of confidence has set in.*

2. Only public expenditures are shown in figure 3-10. Private investment would be of greater magnitude. Private households living in Boston spend an average of $2,500 per year on housing, or a total of over half a billion dollars. The recommended public expenditures are merely intended to bridge the gap ($30 million or about 6 percent of private outlays) where the private market system is stretched beyond its means. Even for declining areas, the proposed programs commit less assistance than the households are currently themselves allocating toward housing.[35]

35. These program cost estimates sidestep dealing with the fact that most lower- and moderate-income households currently spend well over one-quarter of their income on housing. To deal with the "excessive" housing cost/income ratios as well as boosting the housing purchasing power of these households widens the gap requiring public resources to the point where it is probably unbridgeable.

3. This analysis does not attempt to deal with the complexities and nuances of current public housing assistance strategies, except to point out that the current forms of supply-oriented subsidies cost more per unit, and recent indications suggest they are less cost effective in the long run than those proposed here, largely because assisted construction tends to lock disadvantaged families together into clusters undermining neighborhood confidence. Granting the subsidies directly to eligible households (coupled with code enforcement to assure that they are spent on adequate housing) offers the individual households potentially more choice.

4. Large-scale disinvestment and abandonment of housing were not generally anticipated ten years ago. Their increasing prevalence today suggest that there are fundamental deficiencies in the current socioeconomic system as well as in past symptom-oriented strategies to improve housing. Different socioeconomic groups increasingly sorted themselves out geographically by different life styles—middle class into suburbia, and the swelling number of welfare dependents into poor white enclaves and ghettoes. The departure of middle-class households and the exaggerated reaction to the potential spread of the poor shaped the city's areas of declining demand and polarized tenant-landlord relations. These areas are becoming increasingly unable to support themselves and threaten to require even more subsidies and resource transfusions unless the basic pattern of human settlement can be altered. Public policy must channel and mix housing demand into residential patterns that are more inherently self-supporting.

The key issues facing the city are not what to do about the thousand houses abandoned each year (a rate of less than 1 percent per year), but how to constrain and control potential disinvestment trends that currently affect areas containing less than one-sixth of the stock (but likely ultimately to destroy this sixth in the next fifteen years). Inaction is likely to allow the contagion of disinvestment to spread so that several years hence, one-fifth, then one-fourth of the housing stock is threatened.

In the long run, new means to redirect migration and settlement patterns are required which maintain neighborhoods in such a way that available resources match or exceed the need for publicly supported services and assistance. The ability to pay for and to sustain adequate housing is too weak on the part of a small but critical number of households. Short of substantial direct public assistance to the affected households—probably a pass-through of federal funds —there is little that the city of Boston can do to aid them. And to do less than the $30 million annually recommended in this book only perpetrates the illusion that enough is being done.

In the shorter run, maintaining currently stable neighborhoods should take priority because modest resources can preserve valuable existing stock for continued future use by all Boston's households. Since this is all that currently available housing resources permit, such policy will clearly preserve more units in these neighborhoods than in areas of outright decline. However, direct assistance to the household, *not the housing*, in areas of disinvestment is required now so that these households, wherever they stay or move, do not reflect a spread of blight.

✳ *Chapter 4*

Citywide Housing Strategies

The prior chapter outlined a series of neighborhood housing strategies. To carry these out effectively, however, certain programs must be designed on a citywide basis.
Citywide programs and neighborhood strategies are highly comple-
mentary; one would be greatly diminished without the other. In
fact, they interface at so many points that each set is essential to
the success of the other. For instance, much housing fix-up will be
carried out by homeowners and landlords only if credit for improvement loans and mortgages is available to them. Code enforcement will result in lasting improvement only if it is redesigned to be
service-oriented, rather than enforcement-oriented.

Four principal policy areas require citywide attention: (1) the
availability of housing credit, (2) real estate taxes, (3) reorientation
of housing services, and (4) reorganization of municipal agencies
with responsibilities for housing. Because several of these issues
have surfaced in the past in Boston without any significant changes
being effected, not only will needed new policies and programs be
indicated, but explanations will be provided why they have not
been implemented in the past and, in light of such analysis, whether
and how their implementation might be realized.

HOUSING CREDIT

The availability of credit for mortgages and home improvement
loans is critical to the survival and maintenance of the city's housing. Most housing purchases and improvements are financed through

69

private financial institutions: banks, mortgage companies, finance companies, life insurance companies, etc. Credit from these institutions is the lifeblood of any housing market. Without it, sellers are unable to turn over their property; prospective buyers, be they individual homeowners or large landlords, are unable to purchase; and no one is able to refinance his property. Without credit, a housing market stagnates, property values decline and property conditions deteriorate.[1] The price of existing housing is primarily a function of the residents' ability to pay, and credit formulae serve to translate long term income streams into lump sum sales prices.

The maintenance and upgrading program for housing described in the preceding chapter can succeed only if private credit is available in Boston. On the other hand, since much of the housing stock in the city is in basically good condition, the possibilities for fix-up would be even more promising if adequate private financing were made available.

It appears, however, that credit is drying up in many of Boston's older neighborhoods. Even before tight money slowed mortgage lending during the spring of 1973, and brought it to almost a complete halt a year later, residents of Dorchester, Jamaica Plain, and other older neighborhoods in Boston reported that a number of credit-worthy prospective home purchasers were unable to buy because they could not obtain mortgages from any bank. In hindsight, they allege they were redlined.

Problematic Lending Practices

To begin to understand the extent of the credit problem requires at least a brief examination of a number of its interlocking aspects: spiralling interest rates, worldwide scramble for capital, and the trends toward large-scale and wholesaling credit, along with redlining and the conservative and limited viewpoint from which banks see their responsibilities and risks. After discussing these various aspects briefly, we describe the nature of thrift institutions in Boston and turn to recommendations for improving the availability of credit. Since housing credit problems are beginning to affect nearly everyone, the chances for resolution are improved, but their complexity confounds easy answers.

1. Sensitivity of the housing market to credit is evident from the association between higher interest rates, lower housing sales prices, and reduced volume of sales. The monthly allocation of each household towards housing can be viewed as relatively fixed: as mortgage terms become less favorable to the borrower, the same monthly outlay amortizes a smaller mortgage. As sales prices then drop, owners with some flexibility become less inclined to sell until the situation reverses.

Interest rates are currently far higher than a few years ago due to worldwide inflation. Even ordinary citizens have learned to "disintermediate," that is, to withdraw their savings from conventional thrift institutions and to put them into investments yielding much better returns such as U.S. Treasury bills, certificates of deposit, and new floating credit offerings that guarantee very favorable returns to investors with as little as $5,000. This phenomenon is quite recent and possibly only temporary, but it is so pronounced that it masks many of the other critical aspects of the credit problem. Lenders often claim that "disintermediation" is the key problem and deny red-lining.[2]

Dollars borrowed during a period of inflation can be paid back in "cheaper dollars" in the future, but lower income households are less aware of this. To sophisticated borrowers, a 9 or 10 percent mortgage today on good property still seems a sound investment; but less sophisticated borrowers recall that a few years ago 6 percent seemed astronomical, and to them current rates seem like usury. They would not borrow at these rates *even if* offered financing. Thus the new economic context inherently discriminates against less sophisticated persons.

Thrift institutions are changing from responsive neighborhood banks who know their customers by name and view particular neighborhoods as "their turf" (both in receiving deposits and extending credit) to larger-scale downtown computerized institutions that compete for depositors' dollars in order to invest anywhere that high yield/low risk returns are available. These institutions favor larger loans, and investments other than residential lending are beginning to increase as proportions of their portfolios.

As featured recently in the lender's trade periodical, "Savings and Loan News":

Red-lining goes by many definitions:
Some say it means no home loans at all to any applicant on any property within a well-defined area.
Others see it as setting the same boundaries for strictly limiting conventional loans or going no other way than through FHA.
Still others go far beyond these definitions. Home mortgage red-lining, they say, is essentially a figurative term and far more subtle than the specter of street maps lined off with red crayons.
Red-lining, say some critics, is a state of mind that arbitrarily sees anything old as not being good. Thus, it is charged, properties in deteriorating,

2. While this seems only partly true, complete mortgage and deposit disclosure is necessary to verify this claim—and lenders have staunchly resisted full disclosure.

changing or still viable neighborhoods which have seen better days are written off as poor financing risks.

Where risks are taken, other critics complain, they ordinarily involve higher down payments, higher interest rates and shorter maturities than the terms set down for loans made in suburbia.[3]

A number of Boston's neighborhoods appear red-lined by these criteria. Recent studies suggest lenders are restricting home loan credit because they believe the areas will decline although active housing demand is still present.[4] Thereby, bankers are inadvertently contributing to neighborhood deterioration because potential buyers are discouraged, effective housing demand declines, and neighborhood prices fall in the manner of a self-fulfilling prophecy.

The charters of savings and loans associations spell out their responsibility for meeting credit needs of their host communities, but Boston has few of these. The dominant thrift institutions in the city and its metropolitan area are mutual savings banks whose defined goal is to earn the highest profit commensurate with risk. Reinvesting their resources in the communities where their depositors live (to help protect their depositors' own investments, their homes) is not seen as an obligation, and is narrowly evaluated economically. Some suburban banks readily finance absentee owners in Boston who already have property as collateral, unaware that this increases absentee ownership and undermines *all* further investment throughout the neighborhood.[5]

Fully-insured out-of-state lending has increasingly replaced residential lending in the portfolios of many thrift institutions. Export of capital is harmful when it short-changes local credit needs.

---

3. William T. Marshall, "The Urban Disinvestment Dilemma," *Savings and Loan News*, June 1974, p. 38.

4. For example, in a recent M.I.T. planning thesis the lending patterns of one Boston savings bank for three years, 1971-1973, were closely examined. A clear pattern of "red-lining" emerged. Whereas the aggregate lending level was fairly constant for the three years and mortgages given in certain portions of the city remained stable, there was an almost absolute line beyond which no mortgages were granted. Significantly, that line corresponds almost exactly to a demographic map of the city which portrays the concentrations of the black and low-income populations. For further details see Randy Keith Vereen, *The Role of Thrift Institutions in Boston's Housing Markets* (May 1974), master's thesis.

5. Tenants, who have been consistently paying over 35% of their income for housing, are screened out from ownership because of inadequate income, even where it would lower their housing costs, because principal and interest and taxes would still exceed the "25% of income" rule of thumb. In the past such tenants often took over the owner's functions as the owner aged. Frequently they took title without a broker's commission. Under recent bank norms, this traditional succession pattern no longer obtains, allowing other interests to enter the neighborhood.

Types of Lenders and Emerging
Lending Patterns

To deal with credit problems it is important to understand the local lending system. In most cities savings and loan institutions are the dominant residential lenders and in many urban areas mortgage brokers have become major actors. The FHA scandals in Detroit and Chicago, where hundreds of homes now stand foreclosed and abandoned, reveal how disastrous the combination of FHA fully insured mortgages and mortgage brokers can be.[6]

In Boston funds for the financing of housing and real estate are derived from three major types of thrift institutions: state-chartered mutual savings banks, state-chartered cooperative banks, and federally-chartered savings and loan associations. Figure 4-1, which shows the relative size of mortgage holdings for these three groups of institutions, indicates that mutual savings banks are by far the largest. An analysis of the investments of these banks based on a review of their annual reports[7] points up the emergence of some important trends: (1) the real estate market is coming to be dominated by a limited number of larger banks in each of the three types of lending institutions; (2) an increasing level of investment is moving from central city mortgages to out-of-state loans and to loans for other than real estate purposes.

Three major mutual savings banks hold 53 percent of all Boston savings bank assets, and eight account for more than 90 percent of the total combined assets. By themselves these characteristics may have little negative impact. However, to the extent that a bank becomes larger, it appears to lose its sense of commitment to any particular community and to substitute computer norms for the former personalized business acumen.[8]

The large institutions invest a smaller percentage of assets in conventional residential loans than the smaller ones. The larger ones also tend to have a more significant proportion of their assets in out-of-state FHA and VA loans (see table 4-1). Because out-of-state loans are originated by a lender in another state, the Boston banks which purchase them do not evaluate them on an individual basis.

6. See Leonard Downie, *Mortgage on America* (New York: Praeger, 1974), and Brian Boyer, *Cities Destroyed for Cash* (Chicago: Follett, 1973), for two very critical views on this national issue.
7. Available in Massachusetts from the State Bank Commissioner's office.
8. This trend was noted in a more detailed analysis of the investment patterns of two Boston savings banks. In both cases the overall assets of the bank had increased and real estate investment in the downtown and suburban areas of the Boston SMSA had increased, but the level of investment in the surrounding neighborhoods had simply remained constant. (See Vereen, *The Role of Thrift Institutions in Boston's Housing Market*, Chapter III, pp. 51–68.)

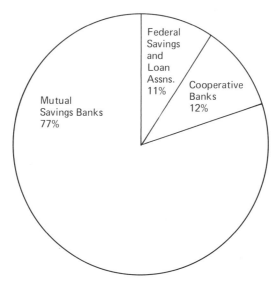

Note: The mutual savings banks and cooperative banks are state-regulated institutions in Massachusetts, which is unusual compared to most other areas. Total assets in mortgages amounted to over $3.8 billion.

Source: Office of Massachusetts State Bank Commission.

Figure 4-1. Relative Size of Mortgage Holdings of Major Types of Thrift Institutions in Boston (as of October 31, 1974)

They do not function as the mortgage-makers; instead, they operate as investors dealing through mortgage brokers, simply seeking the highest yield. Their selection criterion for the out-of-state loans is solely yield, since the government backing of these mortgages removes the risk of direct financial loss in case of foreclosure. While the three largest Boston savings banks account for 53 percent of the combined assets of all Boston-based savings banks, they have fully 62 percent of the out-of-state loans and only 42 percent of the in-state loans held by savings banks in Boston. Any increase in this trend toward out-of-state investments would have very serious consequences on the Boston mortgage market. The first result would be a fund drain; i.e., money deposited in Boston would supply mortgages in other states at the expense of Boston area residents. Secondly, financial institutions might move out of the local mortgage market entirely, being content merely to purchase and sell mortgages originated elsewhere much as they would any other type of liquid asset. Thirdly, mortgage brokers might then move into the local

Table 4-1. Loan Picture of Major Boston Savings Banks (as of Dec. 31, 1974)

Savings Banks	Total Assets in millions	Total Real Estate Loans	Total Real Estate Loans as % of Total Assets	Total GI & FHA Loans $millions	% of Total Real Estate Loans	In-State GI & FHA Loans $millions	% of Total GI & FHA Loans	Conventional Loans $millions	% of Total Real Estate Loans
Boston Five	$815.1	$608.4	74.6%	$319.6	52.5%	$113.1	35.4%	$288.8	47.5%
Charlestown	670.4	411.6	61.4	128.8	31.3	51.6	40.1	282.8	68.7
Dorchester	252.6	195.1	77.2	51.8	26.6	30.8	59.5	143.3	73.4
East Boston	104.2	74.8	71.8	35.3	47.2	11.9	33.7	39.5	52.8
Eliot	59.1	30.1	50.9	1.1	6.8	1.1	100.0	29.0	93.2
Grove Hall	40.4	23.9	59.2	4.8	20.1	3.7	77.1	19.1	79.9
Hibernia	24.5	17.1	69.8	1.9	11.1	1.0	52.6	15.2	88.9
Home Savings	348.0	295.3	84.9	169.5	57.4	142.7	84.2	125.8	42.6
Hyde Park	63.5	18.4	29.0	9.3	50.5	5.0	53.8	9.1	49.5
Lincoln	7.0	4.9	70.0	0.6	4.4	0.6	100.0	4.3	95.6
Provident	836.3	533.8	63.8	261.8	49.0	152.7	58.3	272.0	51.0
South Boston	271.3	167.3	61.7	65.6	39.2	11.6	17.7	101.7	60.8
Suffolk Franklin	526.7	345.5	65.6	146.7	42.5	50.3	34.3	198.8	57.5
Union Warren	290.3	197.8	68.1	101.8	51.5	19.3	19.0	96.0	48.5

Source: State Bank Commission Data

market and become much more common in Boston. The shift to mortgage companies would be detrimental because they are less responsive than the financial institutions they replace.[9]

Boston's mortgage market has recently been altered by the introduction of the state's first independent mortgage company, Malmart. Like all mortgage companies, it issues FHA-insured mortgages to homebuyers but then sells the mortgages to regional savings banks, which also provided the company's initial operating capital by buying its preferred stock. Malmark is a new "middle man" between borrowers and lenders in Boston.

Local banks have helped create Malmart Mortgage Co. for two reasons: (1) Malmart is not viewed as a competitor, since most local lenders neither want to process mortgages under FHA-insurance programs (particularly since their experience with BBURG) nor do they want to deal with low-income homebuyers. (2) Out-of-state FHA and VA insured mortgages are purchased by Boston banks regularly. They are willing to do the same for in-state mortgages as long as Malmart will take on problems involved in issuing and servicing such mortgages.

Malmart is extending FHA-insured credit to homebuyers in neighborhoods which most Boston lenders appear to avoid as too "high risk" for conventional mortgages. "FHA-insured mortgages only" discourages many would-be buyers from ever applying. Not only does it raise worries in the minds of these potential buyers, but applications take up to three months (instead of weeks) for processing, and requirements like de-leading are virtually automatically enforced (they can be waived in conventional downpayment loans), and there is no real possibility of "hold-backs" allowing the buyers to make repairs and improvements on his own after he takes title—which is often what makes an existing house a bargain to a handy buyer. Ever since the FHA abuses in Detroit, the seller to an FHA mortgagor must essentially make all repairs and often eliminate all traces of lead-based paint before sale, imposing costs upon the seller not borne by sellers in conventional markets. In addition to the delays and repair costs, the seller must also pay several points to the lender (he does not receive the full amount of the mortgage) to cover the difference between FHA allowable maximum interest (currently

9. In Chicago and Detroit the dominant local lenders—the savings and loan institutions—increasingly sought FHA mortgage insurance protection in older neighborhoods. As these became "FHA only neighborhoods," mortgage brokers entered the scene and took over lending in "marginal" areas. In Chicago it is alleged that mortgage brokers' practices are the most detrimental to neighborhood preservation.

8%) and market rate, which further inflates borrowing costs in the majority of cases when the mortgage is discharged before maturity.

Moreover, more mortgage brokers could easily become a source of further problems. Mortgage brokers flourish in other cities as intermediaries between private lending institutions and homeowners, screening the lenders' involvement in any particular transaction. Although mortgage brokers can serve a useful function in keeping mortgage monies available, they are not publicly regulated like the thrift institutions. Banks are more comparable to public utilities, whereas mortgage brokerage and service companies resemble private corporations. The public has great leverage, were it to exercise it, over the lending policies of thrift institutions (which are essentially state and federally created monopolies), but very little over mortgage brokers.

Boston has an unusual opportunity to influence lending policies of the dominant lenders, but this must be done with care to avoid driving the mortgage business to less responsive and less regulatable corporations. Of the mortgages held by Boston-based thrift institutions, 89 percent are in state-chartered institutions. On a state-wide basis, 75 percent of all mortgages are held by state-chartered institutions. This is quite different from the pattern in most areas of the country where federally-chartered savings and loan associations tend to dominate the market.

Secular shifts of housing investments from inner-city neighborhoods to the suburbs similar to those in Boston have recently been documented in Chicago as part of effective citizen action to counter red-lining. In urban neighborhoods, every dollar deposited resulted in only 8¢ in new neighborhood mortgage lending; in suburban areas, by contrast, the return was typically 31¢ a year in new loans per dollar of deposits; and it may be inferred that in addition some of the urban deposits were being exported to these same suburban neighborhoods.[10]

These adverse trends can be challenged by legislative and administrative actions. While local municipal administrations cannot make these changes on their own, they can support and encourage appropriate revisions in federal and state legislation. In Massachu-

10. *Wall Street Journal,* April 5, 1974, "Playing it Safe," quoting Paul Booth, economist and vice president of Chicago's Citizens Action Program, which reviewed the Federal Home Loan Bank survey of deposit and lending patterns of 180 savings and loan associations. Edwin C. Daniel, "Redlining Reaches Congress," *Journal of Housing,* October 1975, pp. 441–444, presents a recent overview of the redlining issue. Senator Proxmire's hearings in Washington, D.C. in May 1975, are the best source of details on nationwide lending practices.

setts the administrative policies and directives of the State Banking Commissioner are a critical factor. Several proposals to alter conventional bank concepts of risk and responsibility in urban neighborhoods are proposed in the following section along with the premises underlying such recommendations. They illustrate the kind of approaches needed to stop urban disinvestment in viable older neighborhoods. Where market confidence in neighborhoods has evaporated and large scale disinvestment is occurring, the limited evidence available without full mortgage disclosure suggests that bank red-lining was a triggering factor in neighborhood disinvestment, not simply an associated one. Neighborhood confidence can be gauged by examining the ratio of the number of buyers to sellers. As bank reluctance to grant mortgages and home improvement loans in particular neighborhoods becomes known to real estate brokers and owners, fewer prospective buyer households consider looking at houses in that market, while more current owners become inclined to sell while they can still "get out their equity."[11]

Remedial Strategies to Improve Lending

Public Disclosure of Bank Lending Practices. Public disclosure of bank deposit patterns and lending practices is essential if the public and responsible officials are to be aware on a continuing basis of existing lending, and if negative patterns are to be corrected. This information is needed on a census tract basis, and for deposits as well as mortgages and home improvement loans. To understand the dynamics, detailed statistics on yearly activities are essential. If this information were available, residents and public officials would both be in a better position to appraise lending patterns and to exert constructive influence on banks to change their investment policies.[12]

---

11. This argument was elaborated in Chapter 3, culminating in proposed "value insurance." Any attempt to restore credit in Boston falls under the shadow of the Boston Banks Urban Renewal Group, the BBURG program.

12. While this information is not currently collected or tabulated, it is a relatively simple task for any computerized institution to compile, Nevertheless, lenders appear to resist full disclosure, especially of deposit data, in fear the data may in some way be interpreted to their disadvantage. President Gerald Ford signed the Home Mortgage Disclosure Act of 1975 on December 31, 1975, culminating a national effort to deal with the redlining issue in an even-handed manner. The result is an amalgam of Senate 1821 (Senator Proxmire) and House 10024 (Congressman St. Germain). The provisions of the Act include:

1. Disclosure will be by census tract where readily available, otherwise by ZIP code.
2. The Act mandates disclosure for four years.

In May 1975 the Massachusetts Commissioner of Banks issued a model mortgage disclosure directive requiring state-chartered lending institutions within the Boston metropolitan area to disclose current deposits and outstanding loan balances as of August 31, 1975 and annually thereafter by census tract within municipal Boston and postal zip code in the surrounding suburbs. During June key representatives of the lending industry sought a court injunction to prevent disclosure, but a compromise was reached by aggregating deposit data and some of the census tracts. Still, the format on types of loans by area remains a model, and the entire package goes well beyond recent congressional legislation on this issue.

The Office of the Massachusetts Commissioner of Banks has begun to classify the recently disclosed residential lending data in each tract as conventional on 1-4 unit structures, on multifamily, on home improvement loans, and as government insured loans. Boston's research department has examined sales records over the past five years on a similar basis—1-4 unit structures, nonpublic-assisted multifamily, etc.—to identify value, annual turnover, and to use as a yardstick in estimating the normal need for credit. As soon as this research task is complete, indices for the monitoring of lending practices will become available.[13]

Special Credit Programs. Lenders issue mortgages when they believe the value of real property secures the loans. In older neighborhoods, they perceive that values are no longer rising, and fear that loans are no longer adequately secured. Nationwide, lenders view declining urban property values as a threat to their mortgage portfolios. They are reluctant to make additional loans in many urban neighborhoods, regardless of the individual homebuyer's credit credentials, since they fear being victimized by declining or uncertain market values. Bank fear of excessive risk can be countered in several ways which would effect a resumption of lending. One possibility, value insurance, discussed in the preceding chapter, might encourage a resumption of bank lending because banks

3. The Federal Reserve Board regulates disclosure, while HUD is required to collect data and submit it annually to Congress and other officials.
4. Where a stronger state disclosure law exists, state-chartered institutions will comply with the state law.
5. Disclosure will become effective 180 days after enactment, i.e., July 1st, 1976.

13. See "1970 Value of Boston's Housing Stock by Structure Type, Tenure, and by Census Tract," Boston Redevelopment Authority Research Department, April 1976.

could be assured that borrowers would be able to recover the purchase price of real estate, or at least to cover their mortgage obligations.[14]

Another promising possibility is to develop a special program for dealing with the few "unbankable" loans in a neighborhood, which would then render the rest of the neighborhood "bankable." This is the essence of the Neighborhood Housing Services (NHS) approach as it evolved in Pittsburgh, where a foundation-supported special loan fund coupled with technical assistance has been established to assist in fixing up houses to which lenders would not extend credit. Once these were dealt with, disinvestment ceased and more than four out of every five loans have been found to be credit worthy.[15] The Federal Home Loan Bank Board and HUD have collaborated in setting up the Urban Reinvestment Task Force, whose goal is to establish pilot revitalization demonstrations modeled on NHS in carefully selected urban neighborhoods in key cities nationally. Whereas NHS corporations have been started in nineteen different cities, it is too early to evaluate their impact.[16]

A third potential tool lies in a newly created quasi-public mortgage lending mechanism. In August 1974 the Massachusetts legislature created a new state agency under Chapter 846 the Massachusetts Home Mortgage Finance Agency (MHMFA)—to play a major role in urban lending. MHMFA is authorized to raise up to $250 million through tax exempt bonds and provides that these funds may be loaned to homeowners for fix-up and acquisition through local lenders who will be paid for servicing the loans. Current difficulties in marketing "moral obligation" bonds hamper this aspect of MHMFA at this time, but Chapter 846 enabled other important powers. MHMFA may establish lending guidelines and determine qualifying areas, i.e.,

14. Even greater protection would be provided by insurance that covered borrowers in periods of unemployment or illness. A model for this could be insurance provided by the Homeowner's Loan Corporation (HOLC), established by the federal government in the depths of the Great Depression amidst dire predictions of bankruptcy and foreclosures, but which was terminated with a substantial surplus following World War II.

15. The Neighborhood Housing Services approach is described more fully on page 92, footnote #30. See also James A. McNeirney, "Neighborhood Housing Services; Aiding Inner City Areas the Pittsburgh Way," in the Federal Home Loan Bank Board *Journal*, May 1973, pp. 13-18, and Roger S. Ahlbrandt, Jr. and Paul C. Brophy, "An Evaluation of Pittsburgh's Neighborhood Housing Services Program," March 31, 1975, for HUD, Office of Policy Development and Research, and summarized in the *Journal of Housing*, January 1976, pp. 36-39.

16. The joint HUD-Federal Home Loan Bank Board Urban Reinvestment Task Force reports that as of December 31, 1975, there were nineteen operating NHS corporations, ten more were in development, and there were nine Neighborhood Preservation Programs (NPP) as well.

it can reverse red-lining; it can also insure the lending within these areas. The intent of the legislation is to increase the flexibility and resources available for urban lending and it enables the agency to insure mortgages and loans on resident-owned housing.[17]

Technical assistance is specifically authorized, but requires a state appropriation designated for the purpose. This aspect of MHMFA would enable an expansion of counseling and assistance programs modeled on Neighborhood Housing Services in Pittsburgh and Homeowners Rehab in Cambridge. The legislation allows MHMFA to contract with nonprofit as well as public agencies to extend such technical assistance.

A further capability of MHMFA is to act as a conduit for HUD Section 8 leased housing assistance. All in all, MHMFA is potentially a very versatile tool for revitalizing marginal neighborhoods.

Revising Lending Practices. At the present time, Massachusetts bank regulations specify how much banks can invest in out-of-state mortgages and other investments, but they do not contain any requirements that banks lend locally within the immediate area where they are chartered to maintain an office. State and federal bank regulatory agencies could change this policy. If their policies were designed to stimulate local lending by banks, they could, for example, require that banks which do not lend locally maintain higher cash reserves. This would not force them to make loans they judge unsound, but would encourage them to reconsider their investment policies, or, in other words, to reconsider their concept of responsibility to their depositors.

Cities can press for such regulatory changes, even when they lack the public authority to institute them unilaterally. Boston has encouraged the Massachusetts Commissioner of Banks and Banking to

17. Chapter 846 of the Massachusetts General Laws provides for mortgage insurance to be covered by premiums and is limited to thirty times the available insurance reserves, but it allows MHMFA to determine the percent of insurance coverage (i.e., the top one-third or one-half) and types of loans to be made (whether to include home improvements or just recorded loans). A $250,000 start-up appropriation would generate a potential sum of $7.5 million for an initial statewide insured lending program.

As of January 1976 the MHMFA board had still not obtained its seed money, but this probably masks a serious difference between the director and the board. Whereas some members of the board have been seeking ways to commence operations, the director has been seeking additional low-income homeownership subsidies from the legislature prior to moving and it is believed he has not aggressively sought the seed money to date. The intent of the legislation, as drafted, was to facilitate loans that were individually sound but being turned down because of neighborhood factors; instead the director is refocussing MHMFA on assisting those who cannot afford market rate loans, a very laudable, but different objective that ignores neighborhood dynamics.

pursue these revisions in policy, recognizing local benefits in having the private banking industry become more active in urban real estate transactions.

Spurred by the spectre of being red-lined, a number of community organizations in Boston have already become very concerned and knowledgeable about Boston banks' lending practices. They have, for instance, been documenting the "export" of capital from Boston depositors to suburban real estate investments. One neighborhood coalition in Boston's Jamaica Plain section has developed a local investment plan whereby residents would place their deposits in those banks that will reinvest in the depositors' neighborhoods.

More recently the city and the media have joined in this effort to reverse red-lining in a variety of ways: (1) The mayor has pledged to match one dollar from community development revenue-sharing funds to every two raised locally for such reinvestment plans; (2) A prime time TV program, "Jamaica Plain: Options in the City," was aired by the local CBS affiliate and the city planning staff created an arresting poster to boost the neighborhood image; (3) A task force with lending institution representatives as well as community members has been formed to review mortgage applications that have been rejected to determine whether they were "red-lined."

All these measures are designed to increase the latent demand and stabilize housing opportunities in the city by increasing the access of Boston residents to credit. They would reverse the direction of previous government-sponsored mortgage insurance programs, such as FHA mortgage guarantees, which until now made it "exceedingly easy for a middle income family to move out to the suburbs but extraordinarily difficult for such a family to rehabilitate their present home and stay in the city."[18] It is time for public policy to give equal emphasis to making it easier for residents to stay in the city. These housing credit proposals have a good chance of succeeding in Boston, partly because of the composition of the lending industry here. Unlike many cities, Boston contains few mortgage brokers or other financial middlemen who stand between the bankers and the consumers. Thus public policy can more easily influence reinvestment, since it can deal directly with the publicly-chartered financial institutions.

PROPERTY TAXES

One of the greatest difficulties currently facing the central city is the burden of high and inequitable property taxes. In Boston, real estate

18. *Boston Globe*, editorial, April 12, 1974.

taxes represent a substantial share of every dwelling's operating cost, averaging 25–30 percent of rent and sometimes running higher. Private rental housing in Boston bears a larger tax load than comparable buildings in many adjoining communities. While in Boston three to over four months' rent is typically needed to cover the annual tax bill, two to three months is sufficient in nearby suburbs.

The burden of real estate taxes on housing costs has been increasing steadily in Boston.[19] Not only has rent control prevented the tax base from growing, but as the Rent Control Administration has shared its data with the Assessing Department assessments have been revised (generally upwards). The relatively high tax rate has not only had deleterious effects on existing housing, but tax uncertainties have been one of the factors hindering new housing development in Boston.

Basically, there are three major problems related to property taxes and housing in Boston:[20]

1. City revenues depend to an inordinate degree on the property tax, thereby imposing an *excessive burden* on the owners of real estate in the city.
2. Widening assessment *inequities* within the property tax structure result in residents in certain neighborhoods and owners of certain kinds of property being burdened by disproportionate shares of the real estate tax load.
3. City assessment practices are sometimes *erratic*, thereby adding tax *inconsistency and uncertainty* to excessive burden.

Excessive Property Tax Burden

Boston's tax situation is highly aggravated by the city's unusually heavy reliance on property taxes. Over each of the past twelve years, Boston has received at least 60 percent of its revenues from the property tax[21] (see table 4-2). Although on an average basis the extent

19. Between 1970 and 1972 alone, the tax rate jumped more than 25 percent, from $157 per $1,000 of assessed valuation to $197 per $1,000, but has stabilized at this level during the past three years. Taking into account the 3:1 sales assessment ratio, the annual tax bite averages 7 percent of market value.

20. For many older homeowners, and for almost any homeowner who does not have a mortgage, taxes are the largest housing cost. For them, a tax increase is analogous to a rent increase for tenants. Just as tenants have fought for rent control, homeowners would like the equivalent of property tax limitation to halt the seemingly inexorable rises in taxes. This is desired particularly by elderly homeowners who often fear that taxes will push operating costs of old familiar homes beyond their financial reach.

21. The source of this information on tax burden comes from a "White Paper" by the Mayor's Office, "Boston's Tax Strategy; the Fiscal Experience of the City," May, 1974.

Table 4-2. Boston's Municipal Revenue Yield by Source and Year (General Revenues Only)

Year	Thousands of Dollars			Percent Composition	
	Total Revenues	Property Tax	Other Sources	Property Tax	Other Sources
1960	$194,981	$147,578	$47,403	75.7%	24.3%
1961	200,067	147,671	52,396	73.8	26.2
1962	208,286	145,297	62,989	69.8	30.2
1963	198,340	145,298	53,042	73.3	26.7
1964	201,708	138,720	62,988	68.8	31.2
1965	237,836	171,350	66,486	72.0	28.0
1966	254,223	152,257	101,966	59.9	40.1
1967	291,809	180,352	111,457	61.8	38.2
1968	317,013	302,102	113,911	64.1	35.9
1969	326,240	230,896	95,344	70.8	29.2
1970	364,765	253,546	111,219	69.5	30.5
1971	418,090	293,758	124,332	70.3	29.7
1972	499,123	337,478	161,645	67.6	32.4

Source: Assessing Department Annual Reports—1960-1970. Preliminary Assessing Department Broad Sheets, 1971-72.

to which Boston has relied on the property tax has decreased in the last ten years—primarily due to increases in state aid and shifting of the welfare function to the state—its dependence on the tax is greater than that of any other major city in the country. In Los Angeles, San Francisco, and New York, for example, less than 30 percent of general revenues come from the property tax (see table 4-3).

One of the primary reasons for Boston's heavy reliance on the property tax is the fact that the uniformity provisions of the state constitution severely restricts the opportunities available to the legislature for authorizing other forms of local revenue.[22] Because of this limitation, municipalities other than Boston are equally burdened. Property tax relief is more than a local issue; its interest is statewide. However, the situation is further complicated in Boston because of the slow erosion of the city's property tax base. Due to the steady expansion of public and privately-owned tax-exempt property, the amount of tax-exempt land in the city has been increasing steadily. By now close to half the city's land area and slightly over half its total assessed valuation is tax-exempt, with 80 percent of the exempt property being government owned.[23] As a

22. Massachusetts Constitution, Part 1, Article XXIII.
23. According to the city assessors, 19.9 square miles of Boston's 42.9 square miles is tax exempt. In 1972 it was valued at $1.9 billion, 56% of the city's valuation. Thirty-three percent of this is owned by the city itself, another 45 percent by the state and federal government, and the final 20 percent is

Table 4-3. Property Taxes as Percentage of Total General Revenues, 20 Largest U.S. Cities, 1971-72 (in thousands)

	Total General Revenues	*Property Taxes*	*Property Taxes As Percent of Total General Revenues*
Baltimore	$ 703,846	$ 169,365	24.1%
Boston	470,059	276,974	58.9
Chicago	787,636	296,805	37.7
Cleveland	158,477	39,274	24.8
Dallas	155,509	80,939	52.0
Detroit	581,427	151,811	26.1
Houston	183,062	80,402	43.9
Indianapolis	166,858	87,010	52.1
Los Angeles	644,399	190,051	29.5
Memphis	103,931	38,611	37.2
Milwaukee	184,918	82,353	44.5
New Orleans	136,346	25,956	19.0
New York	8,729,249	2,131,353	24.4
Philadelphia	721,249	118,046	16.4
Phoenix	102,428	16,999	16.6
San Antonio	84,280	25,541	30.3
San Diego	137,902	30,697	22.3
San Francisco	583,632	163,341	23.0
St. Louis	189,197	37,080	19.6
Washington	976,272	141,398	14.5

Source: U.S. Bureau of the Census, *City Government Finances in 1971-72*, Table 7.

result, municipal costs must be supported by taxes from the owners of only half of Boston's property.

The actual assessment structure that has evolved appears to have closely fitted itself around the ability to pay of components of the tax-yielding land uses—industry, business, investor-owned housing, and single family residential—and that simple revaluation to redistribute the current tax load more equitably based on market values would tax some of these components well beyond ability to pay, resulting in substantial amounts of uncollectable taxes. Other sources of revenue must be tapped.

Except for transfer of the public welfare function from cities and towns to the state in 1968 and the recent legislation under which the

---

privately owned. Critics of the Assessing Department dispute whether over half of Boston's property worth is tax free. They charge assessors with overvaluing tax exempt property relative to taxable. For data on tax-exempt property, see Daniel Holland and Oliver Oldman, *Estimating the Impact of 100% Property Tax Assessments of Boston Real Estate* (Prepared for Boston Urban Observatory), August 1974, p. 51.

state assumed 50 percent of the deficit of the Massachusetts Bay Transit Authority while providing greater support for highway improvements outside metropolitan Boston, the general pattern of service responsibilities and financing as between state and local government has not changed significantly during the past half-century. By and large, the range of services performed at the local level in Massachusetts is greater and the prevailing service standards higher than in most states.

Until the city's reliance on the property tax can be reduced, and the property tax can be supplemented with revenue sources more responsive to economic growth, taxes will continue to be a major burden on housing in Boston. Many legislative measures to alter the situation are before the state legislature. These include a tax on income earned in the city, efforts to tax currently exempt uses such as airport businesses, and shifting other burdens like treatment centers for chronic diseases to the state budget.

Inequities

Residential property has not been revalued generally throughout the city for over twenty-five years. This means that neighborhoods where values have increased benefit proportionately because their assessments have decreased as a percent of market value. In turn, neighborhoods where values have gone down or remained constant lose by such a practice. Where inequities have been brought to the attention of the city, an effort has been made to make corrections. However, such modifications have only been on a case-by-case basis, and gross inequities are still found throughout the city.

The differences are so great that the recent order of the state Supreme Judicial Court mandating 100 percent valuation threatens sweeping changes which may wreak havoc.[24]

A recent report, measuring the initial impact of property tax redistribution if Boston were to shift its property tax to full market value, indicates that the tax burden on residential property would be about 20 percent higher on the average (based on 1972 assessed valuations) while taxes paid on business properties would be about 19 percent lower on the average. The averages, of course, mask the enormous differentials or inequalities that exist from property to property in respect to how far the assessed value of each differs

---

24. The suit of the *town of Sudbury and others* v. *Commissioner of Corporations and Taxation* resulted in a Supreme Judicial Court ruling in December 1974, compelling the State Department of Corporations and Taxation to use its supervisory powers over local assessors to bring about 100 percent valuation.

from its full value. Thus not all residential properties would pay more tax; some would pay less.[25]

Inconsistency and Uncertainty

It is extremely difficult, and sometimes impossible, for a potential homeowner in Boston to obtain a clear picture as to how city assessment practices will affect him in the future. Although general·guidelines are applied, assessment administration tends to be erratic, and numerous decisions are made on a case-by-case basis depending upon the negotiations between the individual homeowner and the particular assessor involved. An effort is made to avoid public pronouncement regarding assessment policy, mainly because most assessments are below fair market value as required by law, and even to the extent that pronouncements are made, owners are skeptical as to what they will actually mean and whether or not they will be consistently carried out. For example, in the South End residents have come to believe that reassessments are carried out in an arbitrary and capricious manner. As individual owners have had their appraisals doubled, the abutters have stayed quietly out of sight for fear they, too would be reassessed.

Recommendations Regarding the Property Tax

The most important recommendation regarding the property tax in Boston is the *need for a reform of the entire state tax system.* The three basic housing problems generated by tax conditions in Boston have already been discussed: an excessive tax burden, inequities, and uncertainties. All three are closely intertwined, and ultimate reform in one will not come without modification in the other two. Even if all property were fairly and uniformly assessed, however, Boston's property tax level would still be burdensome. Revaluation would merely shift that burden from one kind of property to another. Taxes can be alleviated only if property tax relief amounting to $75–100 million is made available to Boston to reduce the overdependence on the property tax—relief which not only brings in additional dollars for the short term, but which is based on revenue sources which are more responsive to economic growth over the long term. Further, although certain inconsistencies in assessment practices can be removed, as long as the current tax structure exists, the city will be basically operating under an "illegal" system. Whereas clarifica-

25. Holland and Oldman, *Estimating the Impact of 100 percent Property Tax Assessments of Boston Real Estate*, p. 3.

tion on the one hand is positive, on the other hand it makes the city more vulnerable to legal suit. If there is to be real reform regarding one aspect of the tax problem, it must be accompanied by reform in all three.

Such reform, however, will not occur unless a new coalition can be built which will cross normal political boundaries. The city can serve as a catalyst for such a coalition, but it must go far beyond the city's reach, and particularly include the governor, as well as state legislators, business and real estate interests, and residential community representatives.

Although the formation of such a group may first seem impossible, the time may now be ripe. There is a growing realization that the current system is highly inadequate and that each interest group needs the other if significant change is to occur. For example, the real estate industry has proposed the "circuit breaker"—that a ceiling be placed on property taxes so that a local assessor could not assess taxes against individual parcels of property on an amount greater than 4 percent of the valuations they affix to the parcels. An intent of this bill beyond the tax limitation was to force local assessment equalization. Although the growing pressure for property tax limitation is understandable, implementation requires that it be closely linked to property tax relief.

Finally, there are a number of political risks for those who respond to tax issues, and reform will never occur unless state leadership—in this case, the governor and state legislature—is willing to play a major role of commitment and coordination.

CREATING A SERVICE ORIENTATION IN
CITY REGULATORY DEPARTMENTS

In addition to reforms in property taxes and assessment administration, the city's existing system for regulating the delivery of housing services needs to be redesigned so it is more attuned to remedial rather than punitive action and is tailored to the housing dynamics of particular neighborhoods. Because many such changes have been discussed at length elsewhere, they will be mentioned only briefly and references provided as to more detailed descriptions. Of greater concern here is the question why reform proposals of the past have never been adopted.

The neighborhood housing strategies described in the previous chapter depend to a considerable degree on municipal code enforcement, but code enforcement will be effective only if housing inspections are reoriented from their present *police* function to include a more positive *housing services* function. Under existing arrangements, housing inspectors perceive that their job is simply to inspect buildings and notify the legally-liable persons when something is amiss. Under a reorientation they would see themselves as primarily responsible for helping owners and tenants to correct housing code violations. To effect this change, existing housing inspection reports, which merely list code violations, would be replaced with reports in the form of work write-ups. For instance, instead of merely reporting that a ceiling is cracked, an inspector would list the specific repairs to be undertaken: scraping, replastering, etc. Inspectors could also advise owners how repairs can be done or help them find repairmen and/or financing, as needed. This direct service role has already been adopted by a handful of housing specialists working within the context of the Housing Improvement Program and by the housing specialists employed in the Boston Housing Court, and it appears to work well.[26]

Systematic inspection of the existing stock is useful when code compliance is uncertain, because the dimensions and nature of the underlying problems are thereby exposed, thus facilitating new remedial actions. Throughout many of Boston's neighborhoods, full compliance with every last item in the State Sanitary Code is not economically feasible. This forces code enforcement authorities into a choice among (1) being arbitrary in what gets enforced, (2) dealing only with complaints, or (3) redefining what specific aspects of the code will be more rigorously enforced. The last course is clearly preferable, but must be done in conjunction with the affected interests, not simply imposed by the city.

Cities should adopt a "turnover" type of code enforcement strategy, with the results of each inspection being tabulated in the form of a synopsis of remedial work necessary. Code enforcement can be made more effective if its punitive aspects are played down. Most people do not intend to run down their dwellings, and an objective measurement of conditions each time occupancy or ownership changes would be more useful than inspection at any other point in the occupancy cycle. It would be especially useful to a potential new occupant to know what condition a unit was in prior to purchase or rental. At this time, the sales price is established or security deposit paid, new financial arrangements are often entered into, and repair and redecorating work is considered.

Code standards should be identified which the majority of build-

26. These housing specialists also work out disputes between landlords and tenants over responsibilities and payment for repairs by negotiating the rent consequences. They mediate between owner and tenant.

ings in a given neighborhood can meet and enforcement should be tailored to these varying levels.[27] Universal and full enforcement of codes is presently avoided because it may force abandonment (thereby benefiting neither owner nor renter) or require the city to provide relocation into standard dwellings at modest rents—an impossible task. Guidelines must distinguish between more and less urgent situations, and in the case of the former, develop the rights and procedures for relocation. When cash flow is insufficient to support fix-up, the principle that tenants may face rent increases to help pay for the necessary fix-up must be reaffirmed.

These guidelines must arise from a shared conviction among tenants, owners, and municipal agencies that code enforcement is a vital component in a holding action; they must evolve through a cooperative process among these groups. Cities can do much to foster such a process through setting the right climate where tenant landlord differences are mediated, not polarized.[28]

A six-month rent escrow law should be enacted to apply to any dwelling with certified impaired habitability: certification should be made in response to tenant complaints, and the tenant should initiate the escrowing. This form of code enforcement is more effective in several ways than current means of court fines, administrative hearings, continuances, etc.:

1. The cash flow from rent is maintained.
2. The entire cash flow is diverted to make the repairs if they are at all possible.
3. The tenant can initiate enforcement if he thinks the repairs can be afforded by the owner (and/or possibly himself through rent increases) but not if it will result in abandonment. Thus, the mechanism is self-regulating.
4. The owner is held responsible as far as possible, and third parties (the municipality or receivers) are not confusing this responsibility.

27. Some helpful ideas may be found in Richard E. Starr, "Residential Rehabilitation Process," Real Estate Research Corporation, Chicago, 1975 (mimeo.). A general discussion of tenant involvement in housing code programs can be found in Chester Hartman et al., "Municipal Housing Code Enforcement and Low-Income Tenants," *AIP Journal*, March 1974, and in Melvin R. Levin and Joseph S. Slavet, *New Approaches to Housing Code Administration*, prepared for the National Commission on Urban Problems, Research Report No. 17 (Washington, D.C., USGPO, 1969), pp. 48–53. See also Chapter 3, discussion on technical assistance coupled with code enforcement.

28. In Pittsburgh, such a set of standards, expressed in an objective point system evolved by the County Health Department working over time with a group of concerned owners and tenants to mutually determine what was fair. While this set of standards, criteria, point system, and back-up legislation are available for adaptation elsewhere, the groups involved must first recognize the need.

5. If the process leads to abandonment by the owner, there is immediate feedback. The building can be intercepted before the tenants move out and vandals take over.

Present legislation affecting rent withholding, retaliatory evictions, rent receiverships, and municipal repairs should be reviewed, to determine their actual impact on the fix-up process. Often under such statutes owners are not assured back rent when they complete repairs or are uncertain what repairs are necessary to obtain such back rent, so they often do not make the repairs. If the problem lies in the laws rather than the local administration, these laws should be amended, clarifying the obligations to collect, hold, and account for rent monies. A nonpartisan escrow agent should be appointed to hold rents in individual accounts and inform owners of accumulating balances in order to avoid pro-tenant or pro-owner bias in administration.[29] Owners need protection from "bad" tenants, just as tenants need protection from "bad" landlords.

Neighborhood revitalization requires a finely tuned array of strategies, considerably more comprehensive than code enforcement and some legislative changes. Fix-up is a contagious process which the city can initiate with visible public improvements. Resurfacing streets, improving lighting, removing rubbish and debris accumulations, tree planting and pruning—all these municipal actions, which reveal that the city is doing its part, should commence before code enforcement.

Many owners would then fix-up their property if they knew how, but often they do not know a contractor they trust, nor the extent of work they should undertake when they finally get a contractor. Some people could do much of the fix-up themselves, while others could save much money by dealing directly with subcontractors. Good counseling and technical assistance can greatly increase the productivity of each dollar available for fix-up. These could be provided by the city or private parties. The best way lies in the development of the profession of rehabilitation counselor, the cost of whose services may be included in a fix-up loan or home mortgage like an architect's professional services.

Neighborhood revitalization then is more than sensitive code enforcement, but it occurs when it is approached in a timely and appropriate manner, beginning with public improvements scheduled

29. The Pennsylvania law provides a model. It focuses on remedial situations and allows the tenant to escrow rents for up to six months to have the situation corrected. In effect it is like putting the rent in a glass jar. If the owner complies within the six months, he is awarded the rent; if he does not, it is all returned to the tenant.

so they precede code enforcement, and then dealing with blighting structures while providing technical assistance and credit to home-owners.

The best model combining all these factors remains the Neighborhood Housing Services program established in Pittsburgh, which demonstrates how all these strategies can fit together to revitalize an area.[30]

DEALING WITH RED TAPE BLIGHT

An overall reorganization and reorientation of all city housing agencies will usually be necessary if the city is to take the lead in restoration of the housing stock. In Boston, with at least twenty-three local agencies involved in housing, not to mention various state and federal agencies, municipal responsibility is diffused and implementation of policy often becomes confused.[31] For example, any one of four agencies may be responsible for conducting a housing inspection, depending on the kind of problem. Overlapping authority causes

30. See James A. McNeirney, "Neighborhood Housing Services; Aiding Inner City Areas the Pittsburgh Way," in Federal Home Loan Bank Board *Journal*, May 1973, pp. 13-18, and Roger S. Ahlbrandt, Jr. and Paul C. Brophy, "Neighborhood Housing Services: A Unique Formula Proves Itself in Turning Around Declining Neighborhoods," *Journal of Housing*, January 1976, pp. 36-39. Essentially NHS builds neighborhood confidence by generating momentum and dealing with the "one out of five" unbankable situations, to make the rest of the needs bankable propositions. There are a number of elements necessary to make this effort work (cited by Ahlbrandt and Brophy): (1) *target neighborhoods:* neighborhoods should be targeted based on community initiative for a concentrated program approach rather than diluting the impact of limited available resources on a citywide effort; (2) *public investment:* increased public investment in the neighborhood is required to convey to residents and financial institutions that the city is committed to the neighborhood; (3) *systematic code enforcement:* a systematic code enforcement program is required to stimulate property owners to reinvest; visible signs of investment are key indicators of neighborhood improvement; if some property owners are reluctant to meet codes, a suitable enforcement mechanism is required; (4) *subsidized loan fund:* a subsidized loan fund for home improvement loans is necessary to assist those unable to afford conventional financing; and (5) *financial institution involvement:* the involvement of financial institutions is necessary to ensure that mortgage and home improvement loans will be made to bankable property owners in the area.

31. These include: Assessing Department, Back Bay Architectural Commission and Beacon Hill Architectural Commission, Board of Appeals, Boston Housing Authority, Boston Redevelopment Authority, Building Department, Collector Treasurer's Office, Fire Department's Fire Prevention Division, Health and Hospitals Department's Environmental Sanitation Section, Housing Court, Housing Inspection Department, Licensing Board, Mayor's Office, Office of Community Development, Office of Public Services, Public Facilities Department, Public Improvement Commission, Public Works, Real Property Department, Tax Title Division of the Law Department, Rent Control Administration, and the Zoning Commission.

competing and even contradictory housing service and regulatory activities, destroying confidence in municipal housing programs. The disparate array of housing agencies in Boston creates a bureaucratic tangle for developers and residents who need and seek help from officials responsible for the implementation of housing policies.

The costs of this tangle are best illustrated by the growing but mistaken belief that "rehab is no longer economical in Boston." As agencies such as code enforcement lose sight of their function, deteriorating structures are sold to absentees at prices too high to permit fix-up, but at only two to three times the annual gross rent. As tax delinquencies accumulate, a few "investors" "make out like bandits," but their structures end up abandoned, sapping the confidence of the abutting resident owners and the neighborhood in general. After subtracting the cost of fix-up from the market value of a comparable structure in good condition, deteriorating buildings should not sell for more than the balance, and when they do, it is actually a sign that the city's agencies are not functioning in a coordinated manner, or that the addiction or dependence upon special public subsidies for fix-up has gone too far.

Red tape blight is aggravated by the lack of definition of responsibility among the many agencies. It seems to have been easier to create a new agency when the existing ones failed than to deal with perennial problems. This makes it critically important that regular staff dealing with housing maintenance have the service orientation, and that they not attempt to discharge their assistance obligations through referrals.

Reorganization of municipal housing agencies will be meaningful only to the extent that it can change prevailing norms and institute greater accountability. Altering the city's organization chart will not eliminate confusion and red tape blight unless housing departments become clearly accountable for their work, so that agency personnel become responsive to resident needs rather than simply maintaining a peacefully sheltered existence within their bureaucracy.

Substantial change under reorganization undoubtedly hinges on new personnel, selected under criteria different from those of their predecessors. Instead of choosing inspectors primarily for their intimate knowledge of building construction, for example, selection criteria should emphasize their ability to mediate between tenants and landlords (like the Housing Court specialists); training in skills in building construction should be provided if necessary. Admittedly, negotiating ability is not easy to find and hard to identify, but without it, municipal agencies may not be able to carry out housing restoration. And without it, reorganization may amount to little more than a reshuffling of familiar faces on the newest organization chart.[32]

Attracting new staff into city agencies can be a formidable job in the face of Civil Service regulations and employee-union realities. However, strong commitment from the chief executive could overcome these obstacles and gradually change the tenor and quality of operating agencies. Opening agency decisions and records to public scrutiny—again a form of disclosure—improves accountability and enables citizens to understand what standards guide agency actions and thereby anticipate what kinds of assistance or treatment they will receive there.

CONCLUSIONS REGARDING CITY ROLES

By now it should be clear that housing problems, housing policies, and housing reform are complex issues involving a wide range of actors and necessitating changes at neighborhood, municipal, state and federal levels. Absolute or simple solutions are illusive, and in such a maze, one of the glaring possibilities is that everyone will blame everybody else, and consequently little, if anything, will ever be achieved. If solutions are to be realized, they must come through a process which brings together the various actors involved, builds upon a foundation of common understanding, and works toward the best solution possible given the circumstances.

More open administration, computerization of records, and increased public disclosure of agency actions offer the greatest promise of reform, because they will bring about clarification of objectives and accountability among the actors involved in housing. Increasing bureaucratization during the past decade has allowed everyone to lose sight of his part in maintaining decent housing. Banker, tax collector, housing inspector, owner, tenant—each cling to the illusion that another is to blame, that forces beyond him are at work undermining neighborhood confidence and that others hold the key to improved housing, whereas there is actually a tug-of-war on the limited resources the consumer is willing to pay for his housing. These resources must be shared between keeping up the dwelling, meeting operating costs and real estate taxes, and providing a fair

32. On the one hand, reduction in number of staff as well as number of agencies is likely to be beneficial; on the other, the new community development funds allow the creation of a new corps of professionals in housing services. These could be promoted from within, as models for the rank and file to emulate, or newly recruited, but in any case, new criteria must govern selection instead of simply "rewarding the faithful" if city housing services are going to meet the challenges that lie ahead.

return to the owner. When these resources are scant, and tax collector and owner both try to skim what they can, the dwelling suffers.

Neighborhood confidence, however, is fundamental to this sytem. When confidence is high, willingness to pay and invest is firm; and as confidence ebbs, less resources go into the system, causing a pinch in maintenance, taxes collected, and the return on investment of decent owners; and when confidence does return to a neighborhood, it is amazing how quickly the physical aspects can be improved.

Chapter 5

Reducing Housing Imbalances

As Chapter 1 indicated, this book concentrates on two housing issues: (1) the quality of Boston's housing, and (2) the
mix of housing opportunities for various income groups
both among neighborhoods within the city and among communities
within the metropolitan area. The previous chapters focused on the
first of these two concerns by examining how problems could be addressed *within* the central city, and identified significant efforts
already being undertaken in this regard. This chapter looks at the
second set of the issues, mixing and balance, which requires longer-
range perspective and broader concensus with higher levels of government before the systemic changes required to achieve such balance
can take place. This chapter is more hypothetical than the preceding
because these issues have so far received much less attention. It must
be stressed at the outset that any action strategy will necessarily
involve forces outside the central city, including federal initiatives
which can only be expected to come into focus more gradually than
the efforts to deal with the quality of housing.

Like most American central cities, Boston is confronted by housing issues which do not begin and end at its edges. Frequently housing
problems within the city have their origins in housing conditions
and markets in surrounding communities. For instance, bank disinvestment, discussed in the previous chapter, arises in part from
alternative and more attractive mortgage investment options which
banks have in the suburbs.

Exclusionary housing markets are a problem of special importance that also spill across political boundaries. Most communities

offer only a narrow range of housing opportunities to various income and racial groups; class and race segregation appear to limit choice in many communities. Thus the housing focus in this chapter is the entire metropolitan area rather than the central city alone because there are serious socioeconomic disparities between the city and the rest of the area, and efforts to achieve a reasonable degree of housing balance for the metropolitan area as a whole are thwarted by these inequalities.

Appendix A notes the extent of racial-income disparities between Boston's population and the population of the rest of the metropolitan area. Boston has a larger proportion of lower-income and a smaller proportion of middle- and upper-income households than the suburbs; and these income gaps are widening. The central city, containing only a quarter of the total population of the Boston SMSA,[1] houses over two-fifths of the area's poor and near-poor residents (i.e., with annual incomes below $5,000) and over three-quarters of the area's non-white residents. Furthermore, within the city itself, individual neighborhoods tend to be relatively homogeneous in race and income, and there are racial/economic disparities between neighborhoods.

To open housing choices requires redressing disparities which artificially restrict the housing choices of many groups and individuals. Some of these discriminatory patterns are economic; others are racial. Both public and private practices help shape these patterns.

Restrictive zoning and building codes are examples of discriminatory public policies that prevail in many Boston suburbs. Large lot zoning and unreasonably high standards in building codes push the price of housing far beyond the reach of moderate- and—in a few places—even middle-income families. Brokers in the private real estate market often operate as if to curb the potential housing choices of minority and lower income households to the inner city.

This chapter begins by describing several housing-related issues which are linked to the segregation of metropolitan area residents by race and income: fiscal, educational, mortgage credit, and employment disparities. The leading causes of the present racial and economic imbalances *among* communities are then discussed, followed by an evaluation of previous and current public efforts aimed at reducing demographic imbalances by improving the mix of available housing. Finally, new strategies are proposed for reducing income and race disparities in housing between the central city and the surrounding area, as well as within the central city itself.

1. Standard Metropolitan Statistical Area, a term universally used by planners to officially designate the metropolitan area.

HOUSING-LINKED DISPARITIES IN THE
METROPOLITAN AREA

Access to many public and private opportunities in our society is linked to the location of one's housing. Both the property taxes one pays and the public services one receives are a function of the city or town where one lives. Children's access to public schools is usually similarly determined. Increasingly the present or potential access of a homeowner to mortgage credit is tied to the community where that person chooses to live. A person's employment and access to jobs is also somewhat constrained by the location of his home.

In all four of these areas—taxes, schools, housing credit, and employment—the disparities between the opportunities available within Boston and those available in the surrounding metropolitan area are growing. This section examines each of these areas of disparity in some detail.

Fiscal Disparities

Boston's relatively high and inequitable property tax levels and the importance of state tax reforms to correct these conditions were reviewed in Chapter 4. This discussion examines the link between the city's property taxes and the growing socioeconomic disparities between the city and the surrounding area.

The system of real estate taxes began when real property was a reasonable measure of individual and business wealth. One hundred years ago most individual wealth was tied up in land holdings, and most business wealth was in factories or commercial establishments —mainly located within the city. Now, however, land ownership is not the predominant form of privately-held capital, and businesses are increasingly service enterprises, the primary assets of which are skilled people and information, rather than real estate. Thus real estate valuations are becoming increasingly inappropriate as a base for raising municipal revenues. At the same time the inherent weaknesses of property tax administration tend to perpetuate gross inequities in property tax assessments.[2]

Difficulties with the property tax are compounded by the fact

2. The regressive nature of this disparity becomes apparent when one compares the tax impact on a typical Boston resident with that on his relatively better-off suburban counterpart. In Boston, rents commonly represent 35 percent of household income, and taxes account for 30–35 percent of rent, resulting in city taxes consuming one-tenth of household income; the suburban counterpart pays closer to 25 percent of income in rent, and property taxes account for only 20 percent of his rent, or about one-twentieth of household income.

that increases in the central city's taxable base are lagging behind the trends of municipal expenses. Outmigration of middle- and upper-income households from Boston has added to the fiscal difficulties of the central city because property occupied by poorer households appreciates only very slowly, while these households often require more publicly-provided housekeeping and social services than the families whom they replaced. Thus, as the income gap between Boston and the rest of the SMSA widens, the tax burden on central city residents escalates. Among the social service costs closely related to the needs of low-income families are public housing, housing inspection services, the Housing Court, rent control, and emergency housing assistance, such as help for poor families without heat in the winter. Other inordinate costs generated by an over-concentration of poor and near-poor populations include the financing of special school programs for disadvantaged children. To achieve intermunicipal equity, many of these costs should be more fairly shared by transfer to state financing, and/or by drastic revisions in the scale and formulas of state aid to cities and towns. Moreover, the state as a whole should pay for regionwide services the cost of which bears most heavily on the central city; chief among these is the public transit deficit.[3]

School Disparities

Not only is the access of school-age children to public education largely determined by the neighborhood where their families live, but many family decisions about where to settle are determined by their perceptions of the relative quality of local schools. Families who consider the Boston schools to be inferior to suburban school systems may base their choice to live outside the city on this consideration. To compensate for this perceived imbalance is complex and difficult. Bringing per pupil expenditures into parity between the central city and the more affluent suburbs is unlikely to be enough because social contact and status factors influence public perception of school quality.

Several efforts to improve the city's education system are currently underway. They include a busing plan to reduce racial im-

3. Chapter 114 of the Massachusetts Acts of 1973 raised the state's share of the transit deficit to 50 percent. Chapter 825 of the Acts of 1974 continued this ratio of state assistance for another year.

The formula apportioning the deficit among the metropolitan area's cities and towns is partly based on the number of trips originating in each municipality. A suburban commuter who comes into Boston by bus and subway originates one trip daily in his suburb, two in the municipality where he changes from bus to subway (or vice versa going home), and one in downtown Boston.

balance within Boston's school system imposed by the federal district court in the fall of 1974. But this change only affects the suburbs marginally, mainly through the increased population shifts to the suburbs which may result from the implementation of the school integration plan. Even the more limited voluntary busing program, Metropolitan Council for Educational Opportunity (METCO), which has been in existence and slowly expanding since 1966, but which serves only about 2,300 students, places the burden of initiating and organizing on city households and city children; and the suburbs are left with the option of nonparticipation. There is spreading concern that other Boston families who oppose current integration efforts and can afford it simply move out to take refuge in the suburbs as well, leaving only a residual white population to be racially balanced.

The simple transfer of resources to offset economic imbalances between the city and neighboring communities does not deal with more fundamental disparities such as styles of education or teacher attitudes, which may include self-fulfilling prophecies about the achievement potential of pupils because of their race or economic background. Nor does it necessarily mean the racial or economic integration of classrooms. While the academic benefits of integrated education are variously argued, those parents who would like their children to attend integrated or more heterogenous schools, for whatever reasons, now have very limited choices in the public school system. If the Boston region and its communities were more economically and racially mixed on the other hand, such choices would be more readily available.

Residential Mortgage Credit Erosion

The decline in the availability of residential credit and its potentially disastrous consequences for urban neighborhoods was discussed at length in Chapter 4. Like tax-service and school disparities, geographic discrimination in housing credit appears to be a by-product of residential separation by race and class. It lends weight to the conclusion that the basic socioeconomic composition of communities must be altered to maintain mortgage credit and effective housing demand instead of tinkering discretely with taxes, schools, and lending practices.

Employment Disparities

The fourth area of housing-linked opportunities in which Boston is falling behind surrounding communities lies in employment. Recent analysis of Boston's economy and manpower policies indicate that there is a growing mismatch within the central city between its supply of and demand for labor. On the demand side, since 1950, Boston has lost jobs in manufacturing, transportation and trade (i.e., semiskilled and unskilled jobs), while it has gained employment in finance, service, and government. This means that a growing number of jobs within the central city require more educational credentials and professional-technical skills, as opposed to trade skills.

But on the supply side, compared to the suburban labor force, Boston's resident labor force is comparatively less well educated and trained. As a result, many city residents are at a disadvantage in competing with suburban residents for central city jobs; moreover, they are often better matched to the kinds of jobs which have been locating outside of Boston in more recent years. These shifts in employment trends impose particular hardship on semiskilled and unskilled persons who generally have limited incomes and therefore the least access to suburban housing and can ill afford the necessary private transportation to the newer employment opportunities springing up in greater numbers outside the city. Although it is still true that Boston has more jobs per capita than the suburbs, from 1963 to 1973, Boston added an average of only 2,700 new jobs annually, while employment opportunities in the rest of the SMSA surged ahead at an average of over 16,000 new jobs per year. As a result, more new jobs can now be found outside Boston than in the city, particularly in manual skills.[4]

The housing implication of this economic trend is that many low- and moderate-income families would have better knowledge of and accessibility to these emerging employment opportunities if they lived in the suburbs. At the same time within Boston, the shift toward professional, clerical, and service jobs may give the central city greater optimism that the outflow of middle- and upper-income families will diminish, thereby increasing the potential for achieving a better mix of residents within Boston itself.

In summary, the disparities between Boston and surrounding suburbs are evident through the prevailing inequities in property taxes, schools, and the availability of housing credit and employment opportunities. Moreover, such disparities appear to be partially the result of segregated housing patterns. Boston's relatively heavy tax burden and school problems also relate to the departure of middle- and upper-income families from the city. Attempts to

4. The Boston Urban Observatory, *Alternative Manpower Strategies for the City of Boston* (February 1974), especially Chapter 1—Boston's Economy and Labor Force. In 1960, Boston had 47.4 percent of the jobs in the SMSA. But by 1970, this share had decreased to 40.6 percent. By 1980, it is expected to be down still further, to 38.6 percent. Ibid., p. 12.

balance the schools racially and to bring about more interactions among the remaining central city population may be causing other families with the financial means to live outside the city. If restricted mortgage credit is the banking industry's response to the decline in neighborhood confidence, it can only accelerate trends of deterioration in the city's neighborhoods. Efforts to address and remedy these several inequities one by one are likely to prove frustrating and ineffective in the long run. Their ultimate resolution depends on reversing the basic causes of racial and social segregation. In the long run, achieving more socioeconomic mixing in the housing and population of both the central city and its suburbs would reduce these disparities more effectively than tinkering to modify their impacts.

HOW IMBALANCED IS THE CENTRAL CITY?

Boston, like most northeastern central cities, has a disproportionate share of lower-income and minority households compared to its suburbs. Although the following definition of housing balance—within each community the residential mix corresponds to demographic ratios by race and income for the metropolitan area as a whole—is an arbitrary standard, applying this criterion to the current situation furnishes some insight into the extent of residential disparities and level of effort required to eliminate them entirely. The potential impact of strategies can be weighed against this hypothetical standard. An examination of economic imbalance, which is not so extreme in the Boston area, precedes evaluation of racial imbalance which is far more extreme.

What scale of population redistribution over a long-term period would be required if Boston were to achieve housing balance as defined above? Table 5-1 shows the population distribution for metropolitan Boston aggregated by income classes. Table 5-2 indicates the redistribution of households required to equalize by income class the proportions of income groups as between Boston and the suburbs. The shifts would be most pronounced at the extremes: 41 percent of Boston's population under $5,000 (a decrease of 56,200) would have to move out and 61 percent of the population earning over $15,000 (an increase of 71,100) would have to move in. (The suburban impact is attenuated since its population base is six times larger than that of the central city.) While two out of five families in the lowest income class moving out and three joining every five in the top class by moving into the central city are major changes,

Table 5-1. Population Distributions by Income, Boston and the Metropolitan Area, 1970

Income Class	Boston		Remainder of SMSA		SMSA Total	
	Percent*	Population	Percent*	Population	Percent*	Population
$0–4,999	21.7%	139,100	10.2%	213,400	12.9%	352,500
5–7,999	19.8	126,900	12.9	268,300	14.4	395,300
8–10,999	20.8	133,300	19.9	414,000	20.1	547,400
11–14,999	19.5	125,000	24.3	507,000	23.2	632,000
15,000+	18.2	116,700	32.7	682,400	29.3	799,000
Other				27,500	—	27,500
Total		641,000		2,112,600		2,754,000

*Totals may not add to 100% due to rounding off.
Source: 1970 U.S. Census

it should be noted that in the recent past one-fifth of all households moved each year and that a majority of households move during a decade. Thus public policy designed to encourage a fraction of these to relocate could bring about balance within a single decade without forcible displacement. Current constraints limiting mobility, both in the suburbs and in the city, suggest that a longer time period would be needed to achieve these long-term goals however.

Table 5-3 shows the distribution in the metropolitan population by race, while table 5-4 displays the results of redistribution to equalize racial composition as between Boston and its suburbs. Since nearly one out of five persons (18.1 percent) in Boston are minority, whereas 98.4 percent of the population of suburbia is white, the population shifts required to achieve racial balance as between Bos-

Table 5-2. Population Redistributions Needed to Equalize Class Distributions Between Boston and the Metropolitan Area

Income Class	Percent of SMSA	Boston Equalized Change		Rest of SMSA Population	Equalized Change (plus or minus)
		Population	(plus or minus)		
$ 0–4,999	12.9	82,900	−56,200	269,600	+56,200
5–7,999	14.4	92,600	−34,400	302,600	+34,400
8–10,999	20.1	128,800	− 4,500	418,500	+ 4,500
11–14,999	23.2	148,900	+23,900	483,100	−23,900
15,000+	29.3	187,800	+71,100	611,000	−71,000
Other	—			27,500	

Note: Calculations based on table 5-1.

Table 5-3. Population Distributions by Race, Boston and the Metropolitan Area, 1970

	Boston		Remainder of SMSA		Total SMSA	
	Percent	*Population*	*Percent*	*Population*	*Percent*	*Population*
White	81.9%	524,700	98.4%	2,078,000	94.52%	2,602,700
Black	16.3	104,700	1.1	22,300	4.61	127,000
Other	1.8	11,600	0.6	12,400	0.9	24,000
Total		641,000		2,112,700		2,753,700

Source: 1970 U.S. Census.

ton and its suburbs are much greater than are those for bringing about economic balance. For the long-term future, nearly three out of four (75,100 of 104,700) blacks would have to move out to join blacks who are already in suburbia (75,100 added to 22,300). (Since most of the blacks outside Boston in the SMSA are residents of other core cities like Cambridge and Lynn, the shifts would tend to understate suburban impact.)

The indicators of imbalance discussed above are not intended to imply that complete population redistribution is desirable or attainable, but they can be used as a standard to measure the progress effected by alternative long-term housing strategies aimed toward generating greater balance.

So far we have only explored the general scale of disparities between Boston and its suburbs, but the "grain" of heterogeneity is also an important factor. Mixing at the neighborhood or school district level has very different implications, for example, from simply achieving balance within each municipality or perhaps even just balancing the population of all the suburbs taken together. Many towns, to be sure, have their own "other side of the tracks," and

Table 5-4. Population Redistributions Needed to Equalize Race Distributions Between Boston and the Metropolitan Area

	Percent of SMSA	*Boston Population*	*Equalized Change*	*Remainder of SMSA Population*	*Equalized Change*
White	94.52%	650,900	+81,200	1,996,900	−81,100
Black	4.61	29,600	−75,100	97,400	+75,100
Other	0.87	5,600	− 6,000	18,400	+ 6,000
Total		641,000		2,112,700	

Note: Calculations based on table 5-3.

certain central city neighborhoods are often classified as racially integrated when close inspection reveals a resegregating pattern of homogeneous white neighborhoods turning into black neighborhoods on a block by block basis. The methodology for analysis and the terminology being currently used in discussion of these effects are still in the process of conceptualization. The substance of legislation and judicial orders designed to overcome racial exclusion is somewhat more advanced than the development of strategies to overcome economic exclusion.

INDIVIDUAL CHOICE AND HOUSING OPPORTUNITIES

Public policies over the long-term future can help reduce existing racial and economic imbalances if they encourage moves by individual households that will aggregate into a greater residential mix of different kinds of households. This requirement raises two interrelated issues:

1. At what geographic scale should mix be attempted?
2. What shifts in population trends are possible and/or probable?

The following discussion of these issues tries to differentiate between class and racial disparities, though they coincide in many ways. Economic separation is often used as a proxy for racial separation because minorities typically have lower incomes than whites, but mixing income classes raises quite different issues from integrating races. For instance, strategies designed to open up suburbs to non-whites who have incomes equal to those of existing residents differ from strategies with goals for opening up the suburbs to lower income households of similar races and ethnic background.

Anthony Downs, in *Opening Up the Suburbs*, attempts to provide an adequate rationale for economic integration of metropolitan areas. Downs identifies four objectives for mixing population by class:

1. Convenient access to suburban jobs for low- and moderate-income households
2. Attendance at economically integrated public school by children from such households
3. Daily personal interaction between members of such households and members of middle- and upper-income households nearby

4. Opportunities for low- and moderate-income households to escape the disadvantages inherent in large concentrations of poverty.[5]

According to Downs:

> Past failure to distinguish among these objectives has caused confusion about how suburban economic integration might be achieved and has generated much unnecessary opposition to it. It is especially crucial to recognize that each objective requires a different geographic scale of suburban economic integration.[6]

Downs' objectives in descending order require population mixing at an increasingly finer grain. Since breadwinners can journey to work over a considerable distance, the employment objective can be met if some suburbs become lower-income residential areas. On the other hand, integrating public schools without busing requires attaining a racial mix within each school district.[7]

Downs reasons that to achieve the full benefits of opening up the suburbs requires population mixing within each residential neighborhood, and in ways that reduce concentrations of poverty. Whereas the sophisticated logic of Downs is hard to fault, the need to mix at the neighborhood scale is far from being conventionally accepted.

In selecting a residence for themselves, people tend to be very value and status conscious, and neighborhood integration threatens to upset all the familiar calculations and expectations of housing choice. Will property values decrease, will our children become exposed to the "wrong values," or will our daughter end up marrying the "wrong kind"? People strive to minimize all these uncertainties.

Americans, regardless of their actual rank, appear to generally

5. Anthony Downs, *Opening Up The Suburbs* (New Haven and London: Yale University Press: 1973), p. 103.
6. Ibid.
7. The link between housing mix and school mix was recognized in a recent Brooklyn school desegregation case. Judge Jack B. Weinstein ruled that school desegregation was the result of the way housing had been developed and then redeveloped through urban renewal. While calling upon the city's Board of Education to present a school desegregation plan, he also called for changes in housing marketing in order to attract whites and middle-class families into the area. He directed changes in the building, renting and advertising of local housing. Weinstein decided that Mark Twain Junior High School would be desegregated only if housing practices and municipal activities were reshaped. If one were satisfied by school integration that required busing, then of course the area could be much larger. Its size would be limited only by the limits of a reasonable daily bus trip for children. Busing, of course, by-passes objectives of more mixed communities and seeks only more mixed schools. Hence, it is not a way of resolving underlying problems of housing imbalance.

believe the paradox that they have earned their rung on the economic ladder of life, but that those above them have simply had more luck. As a corollary, they appear to consider those of lesser rank to be less competent, and to be avoided; they are termed "less fortunate" only euphemistically. Another way of saying this is that Everyman wants to live near and keep up with the Joneses—he does not want less than the Joneses as neighbors.

Combining these beliefs with a similar acceptance of the inevitability of housing filtration—that housing is handed down to the less affluent—makes most households fear and resist the entry of lower ranks into their communities in the conviction that once entry is gained, the community will be engulfed and property values will decline. The media unwittingly play up and legitimize this scenario when in fact reality is more complex and varied.

Conventional thinking also tends to blur racial and economic integration together and then to confound it with assimilation or dispersal, concepts which have generated considerable resistance. Assimilation implies the loss of separate heritage traits and identities that form the basis of cultural pride and advancement. And dispersal suggests the forcible shifting of minorities into communities at rates that displace existing residents. Voters, already predisposed against integration, are prone to perceive efforts to reduce imbalance as being in conflict with freedom of choice and community self-determination. This means that although increased integration could solve many aspects of our housing problem, the surrounding issues are so complex and obscured as to render substantial integration on the neighborhood scale through government fiat politically unlikely until the links between problems and causes are better understood.

When individual choice governs neighborhood selection, the resulting communities tend to become entirely homogeneous. In heterogeneous neighborhoods one or another type of household tends to dominate the pattern in which incoming households replace those who move out. Thomas Schelling has pioneered in analyzing behavioral patterns generated by individual choice and his work suggests that unless some standards for mixing are established externally as a goal, or "rallying points" to use his phrase, individual communities will each shift so as to accentuate their own homogeneity, even when their separate members have a tolerance or even desire for some degree of diversity. According to Schelling

Excessively polarized behavior may be the unhappy result of dependence on tacit coordination and maneuver. When whites and Negroes see that an area will "inevitably" become occupied exclusively by Negroes, the "inevitability" is a feature of convergent expectation. What is most directly perceived as inevitable is not the final result but the expectation of it, which in turn, makes the result inevitable. . . There is no stable focal point except at the extremes . . . no particular percentage commands agreement or provides a rallying point. If tradition suggests 100 percent, tradition could be contradicted only by explicit agreement; if coordination has to be tacit, compromise may be impossible.[8]

In other words, an all white community may have only four households that would not tolerate one minority household moving in. As the first minority household moves in, these four leave. If these four are all in turn replaced by minority households, there may be ten more who would leave at that point, while all the rest would accept such a mix. However if ten more minority households join the first four, an additional set of white owners decides to leave in turn. A target mix at any point would stabilize the shift, or alternatively, recruiting some white replacement households would prevent resegregation; but without a target or "rallying point," or a conscious recruiting function, the process goes to the extremes.

Bruce Ackerman similarly concludes that benign racial targets to open opportunities to minorities are as necessary in housing as they are in employment and education, and that maintaining stability in integrated residential developments has virtually always been achieved through manipulating demand and supply in a way that replenishes the desired mix.[9] Ackerman extensively investigated past efforts at integration and carefully reviewed the legal basis for recommending norms before advocating them.

Proposed racial occupancy controls drew nationwide attention to Oak Park, Illinois, in early 1974. This Chicago suburb is best known for its early Frank Lloyd Wright homes and contains well-built, high-priced housing, but a rapidly resegregating process of racial change has been moving inexorably toward Oak Park from downtown Chicago. In 1974 the nearly all-white community of Oak Park proposed a 30 percent limit on non-white occupancy on any block in the belief that this would prevent white flight and mean a better community for the resulting future mixed population. This quota was proposed in the awareness that a 30 percent minority was considerably greater than Oak Park's proportion of minority residents would be if other similarly situated suburbs assumed responsibility for "their share."

8. Thomas Schelling, *The Strategy of Conflict* (Cambridge, Harvard University Press, 1960). See also Thomas Schelling, "On the Ecology of Micromotives," *Public Interest*, Fall 1971, pp. 90–91.
9. Bruce L. Ackerman, "Integration for Subsidized Housing and the Question of Racial Occupancy Controls," *Stanford Law Review* 26 (Jan. 1974): p. 270.

Intense debate led to the tabling of the proposed racially exclusionary zoning, however.[10] At the June 1974 annual meeting of National Neighbors, a nationwide organization founded "to foster and encourage successful multiracial neighborhoods throughout the United States," heated debate revolved around the tabled Oak Park ordinance.[11] Although National Neighbors remains committed to residential integration and to encouraging an economic mix in all neighborhoods, legal quotas were rejected as a tool for achieving these goals.

The preponderance of evidence suggests that many minorities would welcome more opportunities for residential integration, but that there are significant and articulate black separatists like Jesse Jackson who resent the premise inherent in white-dominated integration patterns that "we are inferior and only by sitting next to white people, having white teachers, can we be somebody."[12]

Paul Davidoff's continuing fight against exclusionary zoning in metropolitan New York and Hartford identifies the issues associated with economic discrimination, but to date no court has ruled in favor of the hypothesis that each municipality should zone its land to provide housing for all income classes. There seems to be a judicial trend in some states, however, (including New Jersey and Virginia) to strike down local zoning ordinances which prevent lower-income groups from moving into a community.[13]

The city of Hartford, Connecticut, has scored the most significant success to date in achieving recognition for the fair share argument. In January 1976, Hartford obtained a permanent injunction in federal district court preventing disbursement of $4.4 million in federal community development funds to seven suburban towns surrounding the city of Hartford on the ground that these communities were not doing their part in housing low- and moderate-income households "expected to reside" in the area. These communities may reapply to HUD to obtain the funds, but they must first "correct" their local housing plans to comply with the intent of the 1974 Housing Act, avoiding a concentration of low-income groups in core cities.[14]

10. Daniel Lauber, "Integration Takes More than a Racial Quota," *Planning*, April/May 1974, pp. 14–17, discusses many of the underlying issues.
11. The state of the national economy has slowed the rate of change, and significant efforts to combat discriminatory bank lending practices have had some effect, but the outcome in Oak Park is still uncertain.
12. Jesse Jackson, quoted in the *Boston Globe*, May 21, 1974, p. 21.
13. See *Board of County Supervisors of Fairfax County* v. *Carper*, 200 Va. 653, 107 S.E. 2d 390 (1959) and *Township and Freeholders* v. *Shire*, 119 N.J. Supra 433, A. 2d (cert. denied), 41 U.S.L.W. 3445 (1973).
14. "Seven Hartford Towns Lose Low-Income-Housing Aid," in the *Christian*

In summary, economic and even racial integration at a neighborhood scale would be quantitatively achievable without displacing existing residents *if* the appropriate incentives could be introduced into the housing turnover process. However, the prevailing concept of individual freedom of choice, combined with the current taboo on explicit quotas, renders the maintenance of integrated neighborhoods dependent upon tacit understandings for regulating the process whereby one owner replaces another. This is not enough, however. Equal opportunity is insufficient to maintain a residential mix; some form of affirmative action is needed that is politically acceptable, and currently this does not exist for neighborhood applications. Fundamental changes in citizen outlook are required, and achieving these is likely to involve the courts, the media, and to require time. The first step is a clearer conceptualization of the issues.

PAST EXPERIENCES WITH STATE-WIDE STRATEGIES TO REDUCE IMBALANCES

Massachusetts has pioneered among states attempting to open up new housing opportunities to minorities and low-income households. It has passed an "anti-snob zoning" law and has adopted publicly-subsidized housing financing policies which give priority to the goal of income mixing. The effectiveness of these policies is evaluated below as background for the discussion of options which will realize more productive public intervention.

The present suburban pattern of large lot zoning in metropolitan Boston is economically discriminatory. To combat exclusionary zoning while expanding suburban housing opportunities for lower-income families in Massachusetts, a coalition of suburban and central city legislators and developers succeeded in securing enactment of the so-called anti-snob zoning law (Chapter 774) in 1969. The intent of this law is to stimulate construction of subsidized housing for low- and moderate-income families by providing relief from local zoning, building, and other codes which are often used to block the construction of such developments. Relief takes the form of a review procedure under jurisdiction of the state's Department of Community Affairs (DCA) that allows a developer who has been denied a building permit at the local level to request a hearing and apply for

Science Monitor, February 4, 1976. See also *City of Hartford et al.* v. *Carla A. Hills et al.*, U.S. District Court, Connecticut, January 19, 1976, Civil No. H-75-258.

a DCA-issued permit authorizing construction of the proposed subsidized housing. In effect this permit overrides local zoning and building code regulations. However, it can be used only in communities where fewer than 10 percent of all existing housing units are subsidized or where less than 1.5 percent of the land area is occupied by subsidized housing.

The review procedures under Chapter 774 are long and complex. Since the law's enactment in 1969, few developers have had the staying power to survive the many hearings, appeals and court challenges which precede issuance of a state permit. By the middle of 1974, four years after enactment, only eleven cases covering less than 1,800 housing units had completed the appellate cycle and obtained permits.[15] Even with the issuance of state permits, *construction has not begun in a single case*, as local opposition has continued. In several towns, opponents of housing for low-income families have used the state's environmental impact legislation to delay further the building of subsidized housing in their communities.

Chapter 774 has not been totally ineffective, however. In at least four towns (Woburn, Weymouth, Kingston, and Beverly) local governments authorized a total of 1,075 units of subsidized housing under the threat of the law's appellate review. The law's impact might have been expected to grow with time were not the federally-subsidized housing programs to which it has usually been linked largely eliminated. Unless alternative housing subsidies become available, the anti-snob zoning law will have little real impact. Moreover, some Massachusetts legislators are threatening to gut Chapter 774 by allowing cities and towns to designate specific sites for which petitions under its provision may be requested, rather than enabling potential developers to select sites on the open market. In effect this change is likely to result in the designation of remote, unattractive, or overpriced sites, and would probably discourage most developers from ever entering the process. Even in its present form the anti-snob zoning tool clearly will not soon allow very many low-income families to move out of the central city into the suburbs, nor is it likely to create a significantly greater mix of housing anywhere within the Boston region.

A second Massachusetts effort to develop integrated housing has

15. It should be noted that the formula under this legislation only counts publicly subsidized housing. It does not include nonsubsidized, low-cost housing. As a result, many old communities with much inexpensive housing and many low-income families are still subject to the provisions of Chapter 774. They include, for instance, Lynn, Somerville, and Everett, which probably already have more than their share of low-income resident families.

come from the Massachusetts Housing Finance Agency (MHFA), which features deliberate income mixing in all its assisted residential developments. By law at least 25 percent of all units in each MHFA-assisted project are reserved for lower-income families;[16] in addition MHFA requires that another 25–50 percent of the dwellings be rented at moderate-income rents. By piggybacking federal mortgage interest subsidies with federally-assisted leased housing or counterpart state housing assistance programs, over 20,000 dwelling units have been completed throughout the state since MHFA initiated operations in 1968. Of these, one-quarter are occupied by low-income families, nearly one-half by moderate-income families, and the balance by middle-income families.

Five out of every eight dwelling units subsidized by MHFA are located in densely-populated urban centers; an additional 25 percent may be found in the suburbs contiguous to these centers, with the remainder sited in other Massachusetts towns. Although MHFA can be proud of significant housing production and its record of income mixing, it should be pointed out that less than 6,000 units of MHFA-assisted housing have been added to the housing stock of all suburban communities in Massachusetts.[17] MHFA's impact on economic imbalance has been limited; furthermore, the MHFA construction pattern has done little to balance populations by either income or race since they have attracted relatively few families out of cities containing high concentrations of low-income and/or minority populations. Over half the families resident in suburban MHFA projects were originally living either in the municipality where the developments are located or in adjacent municipalities; very few came from inner-city areas. Thus no significant shifting of low-income populations to the suburbs has been enabled by the MHFA program.

The relative impact on population dispersion of federally-subsidized housing under the National Housing Act of 1968 has been similar to that of the MHFA. In the Boston metropolitan area over 20,000 units had been built or rehabilitated under Section 221 (d)(3) and Section 236 programs by the end of 1973, but almost four out of five of these are located in municipal Boston, most of them within inner-city neighborhoods; only one out of five was developed in the suburbs, including close-in cities such as Cambridge and Lynn.[18]

16. Massachusetts General Laws, Chapter 708, Acts of 1966.
17. MHFA, Fifth Annual Report, September 1973.
18. Metropolitan Area Planning Council, *Subsidized Housing in the Boston Region as of December 31, 1973* (Boston, 1974).

An in-depth study of thirty-six of these projects revealed that they largely replaced demolished housing in urban renewal areas and enabled very few of the residents to relocate outside of inner-city neighborhoods. A conclusion of this report was that "subsidized housing programs have not effected dispersal of low-income families."[19] Neither have they significantly contributed to income or racial mixing *within* developments. Rather, they exacerbated socio-economic and racial concentrations in inner-city neighborhoods.

Thus not only have relatively few lower-income housing opportunities become available through the combined application of the snob-zoning act and MHFA-HUD housing assistance subsidies, but these programs have failed individually and collectively to reduce racial or economic disparities between parts of the metropolitan area. Moreover, permits for new construction under Chapter 774 have become increasingly difficult to obtain. As strategies for triggering significant shifts toward economic or racial integration, publicly-assisted new development has proved to be too arduous, too costly, and the resulting projects are both too massive in neighborhood impact, yet too limited in number to have a significant overall effect. In other words, they create a remote world unto themselves, not really integrating into the surrounding community. Not only will publicly-assisted housing production diminish in the near future while federal subsidies falter, but the relative impact of public action remains dwarfed by recent developments in the conventional housing market. The conventional market has enabled a modest number of lower-income and even some non-white families to move into previously restricted neighborhoods, the latter through precedents established by civil rights cases in the mid-1960s. Nevertheless, the typical minority or low-income family still has limited chances to find housing in predominantly non-poor and/or predominantly white areas. While some higher-income households have moved into inner-city neighborhoods of the central city, their settlement has brought minimum permanent mixing of class and race in these settings. The newcomers either move into newly constructed or converted units, or take over existing neighborhoods simply by outbidding present residents.

If significant change is to come, new and more effective means must be found to broaden housing opportunities in existing neighborhoods, both within the city and in the suburbs.

19. Boston Redevelopment Authority-Boston Urban Observatory, *Subsidized Multi-Family Housing in the Boston Metropolitan Area: Analysis and Prognosis* (October 1973), p. 139.

STRATEGIES FOR REDUCING
METROPOLITAN HOUSING
DISPARITIES

This section focuses on future prospects for economic and racial integration. It requires examining the present constraints to progress and requisite changes, both throughout the metropolitan area and within the city of Boston itself for accelerating progress. At least three interrelated issues appear to underlie existing household location disparities:

1. In American society, housing conveys such status that individual households strive to locate alongside their "betters," near those who are just above them on the economic ladder. Housing demand collectively inflates prices and rents in these upwardly mobile neighborhoods and soon gives them an exclusive character. Families with limited incomes find themselves limited to housing that remains, and non-whites face an even more restricted choice of shelter; most of the metropolitan area appears barred to the latter.

2. As a result of clustering together within their own neighborhoods instead of being interspersed throughout a larger area, the poorer households have more limited capacity to press for and obtain decent city services, better schools, police protection, etc., than if they were mixed with higher-income households having greater political influence to secure adequate municipal services.

3. Poorer households together compound their individual problems to the point where the whole situation becomes intractable in a type of critical mass effect. Well-intentioned efforts at ameliorating the worst aspects of their present housing situation frequently exacerbates it instead. For example, calling for conventional code enforcement or organizing rent withholding actions can result in owners abandoning their property rather than fixing it up. The owners lose only money; the poor their homes.

The American system of values, which is supposed to maximize freedom of choice, also allows individual choices to aggregate into outcomes that are not foreseen and frequently turn out to be suboptimal. Just as the causal connection between individual freedom to drive and traffic congestion may not be apparent to every driver, the links between housing choice, housing costs, and housing problems are likewise not readily evident. Publicly-determined housing allocation formulas, regularly adopted in many nations in Europe, are still beyond consideration in the United States. Income-mixing, which is seen as a radical innovation undertaken by MHFA, has been standard practice in England and Scandinavia. Achieving population integration may not be possible under remedies that would currently be acceptable, but change inevitably will come, opening up new possibilities.

The first section of this chapter suggested that population shifts and mixing strategies are more effective than separate solutions to employment, education, housing credit, and municipal fiscal problems plaguing urban areas. Solving all these interrelated urban problems requires deepening the understanding and expanding the range of options we are prepared to consider. The forces observed by Schelling as propelling toward polarized behavior in racially changing neighborhoods, resulting in either all-white or all-black neighborhoods, also bring about increasingly homogeneous suburbs. As Schelling has pointed out, without explicit rallying points or target mixes, integration will not generally occur in an individual free choice system. The present residents must have confidence in the future of the neighborhood. If they see no mechanism which stabilizes values, they will "play it safe" and move. If the goal is to build neighborhood confidence, there is no arbitrary threshold at which a population is "adequately balanced." Rather, devices for generating agreement on mixing goals are needed to reverse the continuing trend towards greater imbalances. Anti-snob zoning and MHFA income-mixed construction represent somewhat separate efforts in this direction, but they are not of significant enough scale, and they do not directly affect most of the area's housing supply, the existing stock. Policymakers must evolve new approaches that increase integration throughout the city and the suburbs if present trends are to change. The time may not yet be ripe, nor the public ready to accept particular programs, but discussion at this stage is the most promising way to prepare for change.

Preceding sections examined the household shifts required to achieve integration and discussed the scales at which such mixing must occur if balance is to be attained. Although the shifts are modest in comparison to normal experience in household mobility, they involve many more housing units than specially produced to date for lower-income occupancy; and even if assisted new housing production could be expanded tenfold, the additional dwellings would likely cluster within lower-income enclaves and miss the educational and daily interaction objectives which should be part of an integration strategy. Clearly, achieving balance on a neighborhood basis requires affecting the mix within existing neighbor-hoods, as well as income mixing within new housing developments.[20]

Simple economics dictates an emphasis on the existing stock rather than building new units to bring about greater economic and social integration. Since land and production costs continue to rise, a new housing unit will always be considerably more expensive than an older but sound existing unit. And sociology suggests the de-sirability of change on a case by case rather than mass scale. Opposi-tion to neighborhood entry is nearly insurmountable when a developer tries to create scores of units earmarked for lower-income families, whereas opposition to individual households seeking dwellings at the retail scale is more manageable, and usually disappears after occupancy begins. Legal support for open occupancy and fair hous-ing practices have been considerably strengthened through the civil rights momentum of the 1960s although the record of achievement has not been spectacular.

Thus strategy to achieve balance must give priority to the existing stock and operate at retail scale. It must include income assistance, counter discrimination and other exclusionary practices, and probab-ly involve some concrete targets. Each is briefly discussed in turn.

Direct Household Assistance

Since low-income households cannot afford middle-class prices for housing, either low-priced housing units must be created which are interspersed within existing neighborhoods, or the rent gap must be bridged by means of direct household assistance. The latter is probably both administratively easier and less costly, and it avoids the stigma that would inevitably attach to any special housing cre-ated for designated economic classes. Supplementary housing or income assistance would average $1,000 per household per year, reflecting the difference between middle- and lower-income rental housing expenditures. Providing lower-income households with such aid for securing better housing is clearly beyond the fiscal resources of the city or the state, but this capacity is available at

20. In new housing developments some limited mixing can be achieved through housing density bonuses—allowing builders to construct extra dwelling units (above the maximum permitted by the zoning laws) as a reward for providing some low- and moderate-income housing within their developments. The eco-nomic rationale is that these extra units add only marginally to development costs allowing them to be marketed within the limited means of moderate income households. See Ernest Erber and John Prior, "The Trend in Housing Density Bonuses," *Planning* 41, 10 (Nov. 1974): 14–17.

the federal level. The federal government has already been experimenting with or giving serious consideration to such concepts as the Family Assistance Plan, housing allowances, and various models of income assistance since the late 1960s. In November 1974, the president reaffirmed interest in such concepts.

Daniel P. Moynihan, an astute observer of public policy impact and a long-standing advocate of direct family assistance, offers the following guidelines for an income assistance strategy:

> The federal government must develop and put into practice far more effective incentive systems than now exist whereby state and local governments, and private interests too, can be led to achieve the goals of federal programs . . .
>
> . . .Probably no single development would more enliven and energize the role of government in urban affairs than a move from the *monopoly service* strategy of the grant-in-aid programs to a *market* strategy of providing the most reward to those suppliers that survive competition.
>
> In this precise sense, it is evident that federal programs designed to assist those city-dwelling groups that are least well off, least mobile, and least able to fend for themselves must in many areas move from a dependent and deficient status to one of independence and sufficiency. Essentially, this is an *income* strategy, based fundamentally on the provision of incentives to increase the earnings and to expand the poverty base of the poorest groups.[21]

Dealing with Exclusionary Practices

Although there have been gains in open occupancy and equal housing opportunities during the last decade, substantial progress in expanding housing choices for lower-income households can be realized only by eliminating "exclusionary" zoning in the suburbs. As suburbs compete among themselves to develop land uses that minimize municipal expenditures, they seek light industry and attempt to zone out households that are likely to add more children to their schools. Two instances of corporate relocation from New York City to large-lot zoned areas of New Jersey and Connecticut illustrate this trend. In each case over a thousand jobs were at stake, two-thirds of which paid less than $10,000 per year. Whereas upwards of four-fifths of the executives stayed with their companies, only 10 to 25 percent of the nonexecutive level workers retained their jobs after the move to the suburbs. According to Davidoff and Gold

Corporations such as Western Electric and RCA should refuse to move

21. Daniel P. Moynihan, "Toward a National Urban Policy," *The Public Interest*, No. 17 (Fall 1969): p. 16.

to suburban communities such as Bedminster and New Canaan, unless they can be assured that adequate land for housing will be available to all their workers, at appropriate rents and prices. As *Business and Society* put it:

"Until corporations begin to exercise this kind of social awareness, they should stop talking about the do-good ameliorative, token gestures they are making in the so-called 'inner-city'. For by their actions they are doing everything possible to preserve the wretchedness of urban life."[22]

To the extent that exclusionary zoning restricts housing opportunities, such large corporations represent potentially effective agents for bringing about a reversal of local housing policies. This is not to be confused with an argument for "company housing"—it is not suggested that the corporation provide housing for its employees, but that it use leverage prior to relocation to alter unfair and exclusionary municipal building code and zoning practices.[23]

Setting Affirmative Targets

Obviously the day when municipalities either deliberately or through legal mandate allocate portions of their residential areas for lower-income households seems far off, and conscious income mixing to produce clustered heterogeneity may be considered unlikely or even incomprehensible. It is equally clear that an individual free choice system will not dissolve ghettoes prescribed by race, poverty or even affluence. As experience with employment and education has demonstrated, affirmative action which concentrates on achieving a housing target mix will be required to produce opportunities for economic integration where individual households seek it. Without such target plans, economic and racial heterogeneity will increasingly reflect historic accident rather than being an element provided for conscious housing choice. And without targets, neighborhood confidence is likely to depend upon maintaining these increasingly homogeneous neighborhoods through exclusionary practices, until they become extremely vulnerable when the present class of residents passes on.

In summary, economic balance in the Boston metropolitan area is quantitatively attainable over a decade if market incentives are altered and sufficient additional resources extended to the disadvan-

22. Paul Davidoff and Neil Gold, citing *New York Times*, Feb. 28, 1971. "Open or Closed Suburbs: Corporate Location and the Urban Crisis," p. 4.
23. Paul Davidoff, Suburban Action, Inc., 257 Park Avenue South, New York, N.Y. 10010, is currently assisting a number of municipalities initiate court challenges to eliminate exclusionary zoning.

taged. The city can do little, in and of itself, and at present there is neither a higher-level governmental commitment nor a general understanding of the need for such a commitment. The state and federal governments are unlikely to replace the incentives that currently shape market behavior until political consensus emerges that such changes are desirable.[24]

STRATEGIES FOR ACHIEVING GREATER URBAN NEIGHBORHOOD HETEROGENEITY

As previously indicated, the city's capacity to influence population shifts and achieve more heterogeneity throughout the metropolitan area is very limited, but it has somewhat greater discretion to influence the market dynamics which contribute to economic and racial imbalances within the central city itself. It has already been noted that these intracity imbalances in Boston, like most urban areas, are great: most of the non-white population is concentrated within a few neighborhoods, and low-income white families also tend to be clustered together, although low-income neighborhoods are scattered throughout many sections of Boston. If present population trends continue, however, these imbalances will become even greater in the next decade: the city's black and Spanish-speaking populations have been growing faster than its white population which, until 1970, was actually decreasing.

More recent trends hold promise that Boston can intervene more effectively in housing market dynamics. Boston has become increasingly attractive to newly formed middle-income households, particularly households that may currently still appear underfinanced because they are investing heavily in higher education, or have chosen a vocation in the arts and crafts. These households can form the backbone of strong, stable, and heterogeneous communities. The

24. Anthony Downs, *Opening up the Suburbs,* and the many discussions currently going on among urban theorists all help toward building such a consensus.

The Real Estate Research Corporation of Chicago has prepared "Neighborhood Policy Guidelines for 3 Alternative Strategies" for discussion in Cincinnati. The three alternatives represent different models of balance, ranging from *Viable Economic Diversity, Non-Interference with "Trickle-Down"* to *Reinforced Economic Separation.* The key variables distinguishing the models are Household Income Mixture in an Area, Racial Composition of an Area, Area's Age and Household Structure Composition, and Mixture of Housing Types in an area. The three alternative strategies are valuable discussion tools but require a fair degree of sophistication as well as the willingness to devote time and effort to thought and analysis; otherwise discussion tends to be rhetorical and emotional.

challenge for city policy is in encouraging such new households to settle within nuclei in a variety of neighborhoods instead of letting them all attempt to congregate in upper-class enclaves—the South End, Back Bay, Beacon Hill, and Charlestown. Overconcentration of these households will simply displace lower-income households.

Moreover, leaving the poor clustered together in areas of disinvestment renders them very vulnerable to exploitation and overly dependent upon public assistance. Lower-income and minority households need better neighborhoods along with decent housing. Virtually all past efforts at improvement or even new construction of residential areas serving predominantly lower-income households have failed without economic mixing.

The optimal long-term housing strategy (which must be coupled with income and educational supports to individual households) lies in increasing neighborhood heterogeneity. Greater heterogeneity is a function of the extent to which opportunities can open up in the suburbs for some of Boston's poor while more of the newly emerging upwardly mobile groups among Boston's younger residents are retained within the city.

To reduce present disparities between neighborhoods, Boston must pursue a coordinated, three-pronged, long-term strategy.

1. Obtain more adequate direct household assistance for lower-income households.
2. Provide effective advocacy for the rights of the disadvantaged.
3. Reintegrate neighborhoods economically wherever possible, using public and private investments to influence this process.

Direct Household Assistance

Aiding households directly is crucial, but the discussion here is only intended to amplify the stress already placed on direct assistance in Chapter 3. As elaborated therein, close to $30 million more in direct payments per year to lower-income households is necessary to enable the 14 percent (approximately 30,000 households) currently living in the declining areas of Boston to afford the cost of decent housing. Extending such assistance to cover the rent gap of lower-income households throughout the city would require an estimated expenditure of $100 million per year.[25]

25. These rent gap estimates assume that assistance payments would supplement the current expenditures on the part of these households for housing and *not* necessarily reduce their housing budget to less than 25 percent of income as Section 8 requires. The BRA Research Department made estimates in preparation of the Housing Assistance Plan required under federal community development revenue sharing and found 58 percent of Boston's households

However, direct assistance payments per household would generally be less than the unit cost of publicly-aided housing such as Section 8. Many more households are eligible for such assistance than were served by past production-oriented housing subsidy programs. Unfortunately direct household assistance has much less political glamour than facilitating visible new construction, but central cities nationally have a shared interest in obtaining such direct assistance for their lower-income population making it worthwhile to form a national coalition to press for such federal assistance.

The links between spreading disinvestment, housing abandonment, and the low incomes of many households, incomes which are inadequate to purchase decent housing, have not been conclusively proven, but evidence is accumulating that it costs as much or more to house a low-income family as a moderate-income one.[26] The extent to which inadequate income is a prime cause in the decline of existing residential neighborhoods requires detailed research, but the hypothesis is strong that if such households had the income to pay their way, they would be less likely to be excluded or treated as outcasts in heterogeneous neighborhoods.

Effective Advocacy for the Disadvantaged

How to aid lower-income households in securing their housing rights is best illustrated by the consumer-supportive counseling services made available to all participants in the experimental federally-assisted Housing Allowance Program (HAP) under way in Springfield, Massachusetts. HAP makes resources available to assist individual households obtain what they are entitled to in the conventional housing market. Participants are informed how exploitation and discrimination can erode their housing dollar, how leases can benefit tenants as well as landlords, what their options are regarding security deposits, etc., but the initiative for action must come from the affected household. Pursuing this approach, the Springfield HAP has not only aided minority households to enter new residential areas with little opposition but has helped families in securing correction of housing code violations through their increased effective purchasing power. Closer examination of the

have less than 80 percent of median metropolitan household income, rendering them eligible for housing assistance under Section 8 of the National Housing and Community Development Act of 1974. However, Section 8 assistance earmarked for Boston is only adequate to aid one in fifty eligible households, posing a major equity problem.

26. BRA and BUO, *Subsidized Multi-Family Rental Housing in Boston, op.cit.,* and interviews with staff of The Boston Housing Authority, Planning Department.

extent and ways in which the Springfield HAP avoided simply inflating the price of housing for all households is critical to replicating this approach elsewhere. At this point only the scope of advocacy required can be identified, because ways of assuring its effective application are not yet fully understood. Sponsors or funding for this type of advocacy may be difficult to obtain because such assistance, effectively administered, challenges entrenched interests.

Increase Economic and Racial Heterogeneity

Reintegrating neighborhoods presents a major long-term challenge, but the city, acting in concert with lenders and other large institutions that affect land use throughout the city, is in a position to have substantial impact on future residential patterns by shaping neighborhood confidence. Chapter 3 discussed neighborhood market dynamics and differentiated areas by strength of housing demand, concluding that public investment in housing stock should be limited to stable and rising areas. The recent national housing policies awarded subsidies to housing suppliers and attempted largely to "gild the ghetto," and the failure of many of the resulting projects to meet their mortgage payments is partly attributable to this policy. In weak demand areas, where there is little confidence, public investment should be more like income transfers directed to households to maximize free choice on the part of the residents in determining whether to move or remain. Preliminary indications of the housing allowance experiment in Springfield suggest that roughly as many chose to remain in their units as decided to move. Direct income assistance is likely to generate greater mobility in the housing market than past policies of building subsidized housing in blighted areas, and the challenge becomes one of encouraging more heterogeneity in resettlement patterns as such assistance is made available.

The city is a dynamic and continually changing system. Many of its parts that were recently blighted have been experiencing extensive revitalization—the Back Bay, the South End, Charlestown, the waterfront, and many pockets scattered throughout the city. Households settling in these areas consist mainly of new young households who are of middle- or upper-income status, rather than households moving back from the suburbs. This resettlement process, however, often results in the displacement of lower-income and elderly households who cannot keep up with the rapidly rising rents in such areas.[27] If resettlement had proceeded more gradually with some

27. Earmarking new subsidized housing developments for such lower-income families in urban renewal areas has provided much needed lower-income housing, but has failed to integrate these households into the rejuvenating community, and herded them instead into projects or enclaves.

planning, new young households could simply have *replaced* others who moved out, rather than *displaced* them as their effective demand inflated the price of occupied housing. The challenge is to guide such rejuvenation to occur more gradually, even while developing critical momentum to build neighborhood confidence in the public mind.

Neighborhoods with the potential for rejuvenation exist throughout Boston. Convenient location near employment and easy access to transportation are important underlying factors. Architectural character and diversity of housing and neighborhood appears to play a major role; general public image of the area also seems to exert a significant influence. The latent housing demand must be influenced to bring people to see these neighborhoods in a more positive light. New, young households are currently moving into many parts of Boston so potential demand is there. But these neighborhoods must be "talked up" or promoted. And if demand can be spurred, can it be controlled or will these new households come in too big a flood or turn out to be merely transients? Many, fortunately, have recently turned out to be buyers. The critical long-term goal for city policy is to channel this natural process constructively, avoiding the extremes of recent housing market experiences in Allston, the South End, and the Back Bay.

Large institutions like the Fenway area medical complex, the educational institutions surrounding Allston-Brighton, the University of Massachusetts harbor campus in Dorchester, and the community college in Charlestown all act as potential magnets for rebuilding neighborhood confidence. A basic urban strategy to achieve heterogeneous neighborhoods consists of encouraging the development of additional revitalization nodes by influencing major institutions to locate in areas where they will most significantly strengthen neighborhood appeal. The location of the new University of Massachusetts campus and the John F. Kennedy Library on Columbia Point in Dorchester are good examples of such opportunities. However, the city must follow up these institutional decisions with strategies to assure that the new does not simply push out the old—that rising rents do not displace existing residents. These strategies include such measures as facilitating condominium conversions without profiteering characteristics that puts them out of reach of present residents; encouraging new buyers to be resident owners; making sure that a complete range of supporting conventional lending is available; and monitoring rents and conversions to prevent exploitation and inflation. These are the same strategies discussed in Chapter 3 as appropriate for rising market areas in good condition. The perenniel problem of effective administration remains, with the added twist being the active promotion of long-term future heterogeneity. Some conversions and possibly evictions for upgrading must be allowed, but profiteering must be prevented in achieving the goal of a stable population mix. In the future, under a broader interpretation of public interest, a new zoning requirement might be devised to earmark up to a quarter of the existing units in any neighborhood for households with direct income assistance; or federally-provided leased housing could be modified and administered similarly to promote a mix of households within neighborhoods.

There is less consensus behind the long-term goal of racial heterogeneity. Many areas of the city have in the past been characterized by multiple ethnicity. The South End is the most noteworthy example, but Jamaica Plain and Brighton have become increasingly diverse. Ethnic and racial diversity is possible wherever the housing stock is variegated—a quality which many neighborhoods possess. The reaction to the entry of substantial numbers of black families, however, is fundamentally different from the past patterns of ethnic succession. Racial dominance becomes the critical issue. Many residents, including many blacks, believe that areas where blacks predominate are likely to become neighborhoods short-changed in city services and housing credit. A policy of encouraging the opening of previously all white neighborhoods well removed from the migration path should be pursued as soon as there is public support and commitment behind it, but this would appear to be premature in the current turmoil over forced busing to achieve school integration.

✻ *Chapter 6*

Summary and Concluding Insights

At the outset of this book, two housing policy goals were
posed for consideration: (1) housing upgrading, and (2)
achieving greater housing mix and choice. In the course of
research these goals were redefined as improving the quality of existing housing and reducing the disparities in housing opportunities,
and it became apparent that the latter—reducing disparities—would
take many years and basic shifts in the structure of metropolitan
government to achieve. The goals were examined on an "if . . . then"
basis; that is, if the quality of housing is to be improved then the
following alternative steps must be taken; and if greater population
mix and housing choice are to be attained, then other strategies
and measures should be marshalled. Analysis consistently indicated
that the improvement of housing conditions was a more attainable
goal than achieving increased population mix and broadened hous-
in choice. This latter goal requires opening up the suburbs to lower-
income families. Despite some favorable legislative measures and
court decisions, the suburbs have, thus far, in many ways resisted
the entry of lower-income families. In fact, the very discussion of
lower-income housing choices and opportunities is difficult to raise
freely and objectively since the subject reveals so many hidden and
emotion-charged dimensions. Discussion tends to become cloaked
behind ambiguous slogans like "individual freedom of choice" or
"balance," slogans which impede evaluation of how choice, opportunity, and resource allocation really function. Analysis of alternative policies to achieve housing improvement was not similarly
handicapped. Housing improvement is a commonly accepted and

shared goal. But the examination of forces underlying housing decline must be pursued beyond the comparatively simple analysis of housing conditions and fix-up costs to a more fundamental examination of neighborhood dynamics and the factors shaping neighborhood confidence. In these interactions lies the key to future trends in neighborhood patterns and housing conditions.

Before summarizing the recommendations and concluding, it is useful to first review briefly recent housing conditions and trends as well as the shifts in housing policy that have occurred since the 1960s, along with the changes in roles within the intergovernmental system dictated by such shifts in policy. This provides perspective for the concluding recommendations.

HOUSING CONDITIONS AND TRENDS

Estimates were made in Chapter 3 that an average of under $1,500 per dwelling (or less than $30 monthly per household) would be required to bring Boston's housing stock into substantial compliance with state housing code standards, if incentives to spur private owners acting in self-interest to invest such sums could be found.[1] The incentive to invest in housing fix-up, however, is not equally present in all neighborhoods. In fact, only about half of Boston's stock is located in neighborhoods where housing supply and demand are in a state of balance, whereas one-third of the stock is affected by strong demand, that is, by forces where prospective buyers and tenants exceed the opportunities coming on the market. On the other hand, one-sixth of the housing stock may be found in areas experiencing disinvestment, reflecting a weak and ineffective housing demand. As housing, and especially heating and labor costs, have escalated, many of Boston's less affluent households have been forced to spend increasing proportions of their income on housing. The majority of Boston residents are spending more than one-fourth of their income on housing and it is increasingly true that decent housing costs more than many households are willing or able to

1. Public outlays to achieve the same level of fix-up would be somewhat larger due to the added costs of meeting praiseworthy but ancillary objectives such as minority hiring, citizen participation, as well as the time lag, greater complexity and frequent red tape characteristic of public programs.

The recent raising of standards to outlaw lead paint renders widespread attainment and adherence to code standards more problematic. Virtually all the housing stock in the metropolitan area built before 1945—probably over three-fourths of the current occupied stock—requires prohibitively costly de-leading by this standard, which is not generally being undertaken. Rather, general code enforcement is being avoided or administered more arbitrarily since lead paint became an additional issue.

pay. All indicators are that this holds true in most urban areas. The laudable belief, enacted in the 1949 Housing Act, that all American households are entitled to a "decent home and suitable living environment" costing no more than one-quarter of their income appears unattainable under current national housing programs, and has left a legacy of false hopes and expectations regarding the intent of Congress. If Congress were serious about this goal, very different programs are required.

While the inability of many households to meet the rising costs of adequate housing is a serious factor, *the foremost cause of spreading blight lies in the loss of confidence that allows unproductive allocation of the limited available resources in lower income areas.* Neighborhood blight tends to occur where too many such households with inadequate income become clustered and the area develops a stigma which adversely affects demand and the investment patterns of owners already present. This occurs both in some predominantly white low-income areas, but is more prevalent in neighborhoods where minorities are concentrated. On the other hand, there are many stable areas where minorities predominate, rendering the conventional association of minority residential areas with blight an oversimplification.[2]

According to conventional housing theory, as housing stock ages, it filters downward in quality, thereby deteriorating until it eventually is demolished. A more optimistic perspective suggests that people filter upwards toward better quality housing, handing over their currently occupied units to those who may be less fortunate, but who are also in the process of improving their economic status. Federally-assisted urban renewal programs of the sixties were based on this theory of upward mobility: to improve general housing conditions, encourage filtration and add new, high-grade dwelling units at the same time that aged, worn-out structures are being eliminated.

After two decades of such urban renewal policy in Boston, it has become increasingly apparent that this theory has overlooked an important factor. At any point in time a significant portion of the city's housing stock is recycling. Some of the oldest neighborhoods which had become seriously deteriorated—the lower side of Beacon Hill, certain sections of the Back Bay, the South End, Charlestown—have experienced a strong resurgence in housing demand, due in part to their historical character. At the same time, some of the city's neighborhoods which were in reasonable condi-

2. The National Urban League's study, *Housing Abandonment*, links minority residence with housing disinvestment.

tion, i.e., Meetinghouse Hill in Dorchester, have experienced a loss
of confidence and are undergoing disinvestment. Similarly conditions in a number of the relatively new federally-subsidized housing
developments, especially those in the inner city, indicate that some
of this newly-created housing already needs "renewal." Clearly housing age or conditions per se do not determine the future dynamics
of neighborhoods: there are more subtle forces determining who are
the replacement buyers and the new residents, and shaping their
impact of housing demand on the maintenance of the stock. It
appears that neighborhoods in which some representatives of the
middle class remain are much less vulnerable to blight and disinvestment, and further, that class heterogeneity often encourages a continuous effective housing demand, whereas predominantly lower-class
neighborhoods have difficulty replenishing themselves with future
residents who can afford to maintain the housing as the current ones
move or pass on. These neighborhoods then suddenly find themselves
without enough replacement resident owner-buyers and tenants and
then the influence of less scrupulous absentee-owners comes to
dominate.[3]

CHANGING HOUSING POLICIES
AND ROLES

Housing strategies of the 1960s focused on physical conditions and
attempted complete neighborhood rehabilitation and even demoli-
tion/renewal of the housing stock. Often, this appeared to work,
particularly where middle- and upper-income groups were re-attract-
ed, as in the South End and Charlestown sections of Boston; but
frequently it failed, and it was always expensive. As a result, national
housing and community development strategies are in disarray, with
reduced overall level of federal support and with responsibility for
policy and program design shifted to the local level.[4] The 1974

3. See Boston Redevelopment Authority/Boston Urban Observatory, "Working Class Housing: A Study of Triple Deckers in Boston," (May 1975), which
examines this pattern in much greater detail. In essence, neighborhoods where
resident owners predominated find that their own tenants, who used to become
"replacement owners," no longer qualify for mortgages. As absentee owners
begin to take over "renting to just anyone," more of the resident owners leave.
Some of the new owners fail to maintain, no longer pay their taxes, and rapid
deterioration sets in.
4. Although Community Development Revenue Sharing, created in August
1974, will give municipalities greater freedom of local choice in formulating
strategies, the price for Boston is a substantially reduced level of federal assistance for the near future. Community development assistance will shrink by
1980 to only a third of the average annual level the city enjoyed during the
1969–74 period.

Housing and Community Development Act contains a cumbersome and conflicting set of goals, and the HUD approval process for grant applications for the decisive first year of action under the new act was quite lax. The recent Hartford challenge of this nearly automatic disbursement of community development funds to exclusionary suburbs will raise the disarray to new levels.[5]

To determine what the public sector can and is willing to do also requires an examination of the municipal housing roles. The central city is only one of many institutions which participate in the local formulation and implementation of housing policy. In the past national housing subsidy and tax policies have to a great extent determined housing location, types, beneficiaries, and financial arrangements (for both producers and consumers) in Boston, with the city playing both direct and/or indirect roles in providing housing services. Until now, these roles have been largely ones of reactor to, rather than initiator, of housing policies and programs. Moreover, several nongovernmental institutions have been overlooked as having a major influence, by virtue of their investment (banks and insurance companies) and development (universities and medical centers) over what happens to the city's housing and what housing choices residents have.

Experience over the past four decades indicates the wide variety of actions which the city carries out, all of which have important implications for meeting community needs and demands in housing. These include roles of: (1) housing investor, developer, and manager; (2) provider of housing-related infrastructure and housekeeping services; (3) housing subsidizer; (4) housing taxer; (5) housing standards regulator and adjudicator; and (6) catalyst and facilitator for development and rehabilitation.

In periods of extreme housing shortage (just after World War II, for example,) the city was a direct investor in housing, issuing gen-

---

Federal assistance varied severely between a low of approximately $12 million in 1970 to a high of nearly $90 million in 1972. The average over the six years (1969 through 1974) was around $37 million per annum, $4 million more than the $33 million received in 1975, the first year of community development block grants. The 1980 CDBG allocation to Boston is expected to be $11.7 million, or only 32 percent of the $37 million average in the six years prior to CDBG.

5. See page 110 for a fuller discussion of the impact of the *City of Hartford* v. *Carla Hills*. The *New York Times*, January 31, 1976, editorialized in "The Hartford Lesson," "Instead of wasting time and money appealing this ruling, H.U.D. would be well-advised to use it as a stimulus toward development of substantially more rational urban strategies." It seems HUD futilely defends its record instead of examining the goal conflicts and setting priorities. Is HUD to serve the builders, the central city interests, or the lower-income Americans? The conflicts must be sorted out before progress can begin.

eral obligation bonds to finance veterans' rental housing which were subsequently sold to occupants and other designated eligible consumers. Related to this role of direct investment is the continuing partnership of the local housing authority (LHA) since 1937 with the federal and state governments in developing and managing public housing units for low-income families, including the elderly. Under this local-federal-state partnership, local administrative responsibility is combined with federal-state financial participation, including federal-state supervision to ensure adherence to development and operating standards.

Another important city function is that of providing services to housing and its occupants. This housing servicer role includes not only furnishing the tax-supported infrastructure (streets, sidewalks, sewers, incinerators, etc.) so important to the basic needs of occupant households, but also the street cleaning, snow removal, and rubbish collection which are essential for maintaining the viability of housing. In fact, the reputation for quality of such municipal services is a critical factor shaping neighborhood confidence and the housing decisions of owners, renters, developers, and investors.

The city's role as housing subsidizer is more indirect than direct, mainly as a conduit for subsidies from higher levels of government such as housing rehabilitation grants and loans, or as an active participant in publicly-assisted housing processes where the subsidies go directly to the developer or indirectly through a public intermediary such as the LHA.

All subsidies have the inherent characteristic of distorting the basic housing market system, but often the drawbacks are not as obvious initially as the supposed benefits. When there are not enough available subsidies for all qualified applicants serious side effects arise. For example the beneficiaries of a substantial rehabilitation subsidy, particularly minorities, are often featured in news success stories, but others unable to obtain a share, wait "for their turn" rather than continue on their own to maintain or upgrade at market rate costs. And even the market costs are also inflated by the general expectation of more subsidies than are ever in fact available.

The presence of subsidies appears to foster a dependence for more and deeper subsidies to produce the same effect—witness the progression of federal housing subsidies that began with insured loans; then 3 percent interest loans (Sections 221 and 312); next mortgage assistance to reduce interest down to 1 percent (Sections 235, 236); and mostly recently leased housing (Section 8) which helps to amortize the mortgage for the owner. A deeply subsidized development in the most blighted ghetto, while heralded by the media, is no more an achievement than "making the desert bloom" through the use of concealed pumps—only there are not enough pumps for everyone, and too many decide to wait for "their pump" instead of continuing to carry the needed water in the old way.

There are other municipal subsidies that are perhaps more equitable as well as less counterproductive to the system: land takings by eminent domain and resale at reduced cost to developers; legally negotiated tax arrangements with housing corporations granted special tax status under Chapter 121A to renew blighted areas; special tax breaks (nonreassessment) to homeowners for home improvements; and property tax abatements for special homeowner groups (elderly, widows, veterans) or excise taxes in lieu of property taxes on housing developments of limited dividend sponsors. In all these instances the full system response to these special incentives—in higher labor, materials, and interest costs, in the disincentives to the "disqualified"—is not considered. If it were, it is likely the subsidies would be revealed as dysfunctional and a major factor in the increasing insolubility of urban housing problems.

The city's power to tax real estate affects housing in a variety of ways. As indicated above, local discretion over property tax assessments can be used to generate indirect subsidies to proposed housing developments by authorizing less than full-value assessments. However, the most critical impact lies in the way tax collection is administered. The amount consumers are willing or able to spend on housing is relatively fixed. As taxes on any property increase, the size of conventional mortgage it can carry declines, leading to lower gross rent multipliers.[6] Owners who were used to operating real estate as a long-term capital investment yielding steady, sure returns, are being replaced by quicker operators who expect to recoup their outlay in five years, and if they can avoid paying high taxes (leaving the city disinvested structures to foreclose on) then they reap stunning returns while the city's tax delinquency begins to climb dangerously. A few operators in this marginal business can rapidly erode neighborhood confidence as they take over sound buildings and "pack them with welfare referrals." Municipalities must guard against such ruthless exploitation which can erode sound housing values unbelievably quickly. Benign or administratively cumbersome tax collection procedures often mask future costs substantially greater than simply the unpaid taxes.

Powers to regulate housing standards and rents and to adjudicate

6. In Boston property values used to range between six and eight times the annual gross rent roll, leading owners to treat housing as a durable capital asset. Recently property values have dropped to two to five times annual gross rent, and incoming purchasers view housing more speculatively.

the enforcement of such standards are becoming increasingly important for shaping the nature and form of the city's roles in housing. The trade-offs between level of code standards, fix-up costs, and resulting rent levels are subtle, yet they are also critical to the maintenance of both the housing stock as well as effective housing demand. When administered without vision of their impact on the overall system, these agencies can be worse than not having such agencies in the first place, because they jointly create a tangle or "red tape blight."

Since most of the central city land is usually already built upon, these powers become particularly important for encouraging favorable trends in citywide and neighborhood housing markets and for mitigating the effects of adverse market forces. To the extent that these regulatory powers are not fully coordinated and are enforced haphazardly by municipal agencies, the city may be overlooking a prime opportunity for improving housing dynamics toward beneficial ends instead of letting unchecked market forces shape the outcome. It seems natural for the assessing department to determine taxes and for a rent control administration to "control" rents, but it often is not obvious to these agencies that limiting rents reduces the tax base of the city or that the tax bite out of the controlled rent dollar crimps housing maintenance. The regulatory functions jointly generate a climate affecting maintenance and new development which the individual agencies may be largely unaware of, but which the city should monitor and attempt to alter if it impairs resident well-being and housing maintenance.

Increasingly it appears that neighborhood decline is triggered by "problem structures." Neighborhood base maps in weak market areas, showing tax delinquency, property condition, and absentee ownership separately, are remarkably similar and reveal that "good" owners are current in their taxes and determined to maintain their properties, whereas "problem buildings" tend to deteriorate, fall behind in taxes, and contain polarized tenant landlord situations. It is not that the "good" buildings have more income—rather, it is allocated more productively for the neighborhood. The proper role of the municipality is to remove or resolve the problem structures before they destroy the neighborhood confidence and with that the tax base. A city that can deal with the problem buildings can avoid the futile effort to spur fix-up in the face of a lack of neighborhood confidence with massive subsidies.

The planning, construction, and maintenance of housing involves a multitude of other roles and actors outside the city, and upon which the municipal government has only limited direct influence. Within the public sector, both the State House and Washington may appear difficult to influence, but a conceptual plan can exert a tremendous influence. Progress can be measured by a succession of steps whose "time has come" and the city can have decisive influence in shaping such steps if it takes the initiative, even though it has no direct control over the state capital or Washington. The purpose of this book is to aid cities in fashioning such a plan. The private sector (sometimes termed the real estate industry) includes owners, brokers, lenders, developers, and others who have roles in shaping the housing system. To be effective, any planning process must respond to the inputs and overlap with the interests of these groups and engage them in the process wherever possible. If neighborhoods are to be revitalized, a new partnership between the public and private interests is required; and a new plan to revamp the public sector approach and market the benefits of urban living is the place to begin.

With responsibility for formulating housing programs and policies shifting from the national to the local level, customary roles and approaches need to be reexamined—a process that Boston has clearly begun. Whereas in the past the city responded largely to federal categorical programs, new possibilities and responsibilities have emerged. With new emphasis on preserving the existing stock and on aiding residents and neighborhoods, certain of the city's roles emerge as critical functions: providing housing-related services, regulating and adjudicating housing standards, and spurring more housing upgrading and development. This shift of emphasis in housing policy formulation requires more sophisticated orchestration of the city's roles, finer tuning of each agency's part and the more effective coordination of all housing maintenance and development functions. The goal of promoting neighborhood confidence may require a fundamental restructuring of the entire present system for delivering housing services. The process begins by identifying the elements of neighborhood confidence. No longer will it suffice to simply execute more housing inspections this year than last. A strategy to identify and deal with problem buildings, coordinating agencies for tax collection, housing code inspection, housing improvements and special assistance, etc., must be devised if cities are to do more than helplessly watch blight erode neighborhoods and wait for the day Congress provides enough subsidies.

SUMMARY OF CONCLUSIONS

The two issues that have formed the focus of this book—improving housing and widening choice—are closely interrelated; strategies for physically improving the housing of lower-income as well as minority households are likely to ultimately remain ineffective as long as these groups are treated in isolation from the general population and without a basic understanding of the neighborhood market system.

Chapters 3 and 4 propose strategies for upgrading the quality of existing housing and neighborhoods, whereas Chapter 5 discusses how greater choice and improved opportunities for housing mix could be attained. Essentially, these two goals interrelate and the same strategies are appropriate to both objectives: income assistance, technical assistance and counseling, and special techniques for overcoming the effects of discrimination. However, there is a significant contrast in perspective between these chapters. The former two concentrate on currently applicable measures, essentially proposing immediate actions to arrest disinvestment and to counteract further neighborhood deterioration until a national policy affecting jobs, incomes, and economic development can be shaped. Maintaining neighborhood confidence is a function of keeping up latent housing demand—the general reservoir of potential residents who consider the neighborhood an attractive place to make a home. This latent demand is shaped by the media, at social gatherings, in board rooms, etc. When the opportunity arises, this latent demand readily translates into effective demand on the part of households willing to move in and able to meet the costs of adequate housing; without it deterioration can rapidly set in. The challenge confronting the formulators of housing policy is how to create and channel this demand in ways that prevent an excess in some neighborhoods and a dearth of demand elsewhere. Chapter 3 develops a newly coordinated array of programs designed to enhance the appeal of existing neighborhoods to new households.

For the longer run, however, maintaining a preponderance of resident ownership throughout each neighborhood is the most effective safeguard against disinvestment and decline. When neighborhoods become too differentiated by economic class, with all young professionals tending to concentrate in some sections and lower-income and minority households relegated into others, a kind of vulnerability sets in. Countless individual and institutional actions exacerbate this contrast, in effect, red-lining and curtailing services in the poorer areas and bidding up the price of entry into the more "exclusive" areas to excessive levels. There is no evidence of attempts to ameliorate neighborhood conditions which have been successful in the long run without restoring a responsive spirit in which housing consumers and suppliers interact, the very antithesis of a rent strike. The presence of the "work ethic" assures the appropriate responsive spirit. In fact, restoring a middle-class presence has generally been implicit in successful renewal strategies of the past, and "success" often meant that existing residents who could not afford the rising rents were displaced. If future public policy is to be effective, the focus must remain on people, not structures; houses and neighborhoods only reflect the well-being of the households themselves.

This shift toward the direct assistance of households rather than housing is only in its initial stages in this country whereas some European countries have done it for years. In the 1930s it was considered, but for four decades federal policies to promote lower income housing intervened on the supply side. HUD's study *Housing in the Seventies*,[7] questioned the advisability of continuing subsidies to the producers of housing, and the new federal housing assistance program (Section 8) is curiously divided between producer-oriented assistance for new construction and rehabilitation and consumer-oriented assistance for use by households on a "finder's-keeper's" basis in existing housing. But the pendulum of national policy seems to be swinging toward various versions of job creation and income maintenance—jobs, economic development, housing allowances, and the negative income tax. These are all examples of consumer-aiding measures and they are mentioned with such increasing frequency that enactment in some form appears likely within a decade. The national Experimental Housing Assistance Program (EHAP), which commenced in 1972, is a radical step forward, considering the light in which the "negative income tax" was viewed when it first entered widespread public discussion in the 1960s.

Chapters 3 and 4 of this book have presented a set of strategies which constitute immediate actions until such time as more adequate consumer-oriented assistance becomes available. Once this happens, the underlying issue of Chapter 5, "how to open up the suburbs," will become much more relevant. In the interim, the problems of substandard housing will be shifting in location to communities outside the central city and housing deterioration will remain a continuing issue until acceptable ways to maintain stable and diverse neighborhoods are found. This will require more serious examination of the roles of jobs, income, race, and class as well as the way lifestyles interact than has been attempted to date. The patterns underlying who buys and who sells, who moves in and who moves out,

7. *Housing in the Seventies: A Report of the National Housing Policy Review* was issued by HUD in Washington, D.C., in 1974.

must be discovered—and this involves new data sources and analytical techniques beyond the traditional census data so familiar to planners. There is an increasing awareness that the future of mature urban neighborhoods is determined far more by interactions among past, present, and future residents and owners than by age or condition of the housing stock itself. Just as a barometer, intelligently interpreted, provides early warning of oncoming storms or calms, indicators of the ebbs and flows of neighborhood confidence can indicate when a neighborhood is entering a troubled period requiring special attention for its survival. Identification of "ethnic interfaces" is being undertaken and just as meteorologists map cold fronts, occluded fronts, and warm fronts, urbanologists are beginning to map and study ethnic interfaces. Planners are just emerging from a period of enforced color-blindness, when it was considered an ethnic slur to characterize special qualities of Poles, Orientals, or WASPs (white Anglo-Saxon Protestants). But the various interfaces among Chicano, Irish, Italians, Jews, blacks, and Spanish-speaking groups all have particular and distinctive patterns in impact on housing dynamics, and understanding the differences between Irish-black and Jewish-black, or black-Spanish interfaces will shed more light on how housing can be upgraded, preserved, or destroyed by social forces. But this will require new vocabulary, new styles, and methods of field research that are just evolving.[8]

At this stage it is important for planners and policymakers to differentiate housing markets on the basis of their relative market strength or confidence rating, because strategies appropriate to strong and stable market areas can prove counter-productive when applied to weak market areas. Strong or "rising" areas, are those where there are more applicants than vacancies, or more households who wish to live in the neighborhood than there are available dwelling units. Traditional housing programs like code enforcement and even such innovations as homesteading are appropriate where demand and supply match, but where the market is imbalanced it is critical to determine whether supply exceeds demand or vice versa. Where there is an excess of demand, the problem is likely to become spiralling rents caused by appreciation. When there is strong demand throughout a neighborhood, owners become tempted to create additional dwellings within existing structures to gain more rental income to meet their higher expenses. The casual observer may hear the symptoms described as a shortage of decent units people can afford, but the underlying problem is likely to be speculation

8. See *Working Class Housing*, and *The Future of West Roxbury*, Boston Redevelopment Authority, which demonstrate and apply such new research techniques.

which is encouraged by excessive housing demand in the area. The public policy requires code enforcement, monitoring for illegal conversions and possibly rent controls, to see that only operating cost increases are passed along, not the increased costs of financing generated by capitalization or appreciation.

In the declining areas, on the other hand, the problem is more basic. Behind the confusing symptoms of neighborhood pathology—poorly maintained structures, scattered housing abandonment, trash accumulation, and even a "tight" housing market—lies a lack of effective housing demand and a general loss of confidence in the area. Whereas the rising neighborhoods are overattractive, declining neighborhoods are *un*attractive. Moreover, the residents in a declining area frequently compound the problem by "talking down" the area, something federal programs and the media have rewarded in the past by giving priority to the neediest. But in doing so, they destroy confidence in the neighborhood and discourage solid resident owners into leaving, as well as discouraging whatever private investments might otherwise have occurred. This causes an acceleration of the decline until it becomes contagious. The loss of confidence which pervades such neighborhoods, however, is a serious threat that can travel with disillusioned residents who abandon one area and shift into healthier areas unless adequate assistance is provided and care is taken to assure that confidence is not undermined in currently stable areas. To achieve this kind of support for disadvantaged households requires the formulation of appropriate new, nationally-accepted strategies influencing the migration of disadvantaged as well as affluent households. Appropriate strategies have yet to be developed because this has traditionally been considered outside the realm of public responsibility. Chapter 5 identifies the changes in population mix that are likely to emerge as well as which changes are necessary if public policies are to influence the building of more inherently stable neighborhoods.

In ways that at present are only intuitively rather than explicitly understood, the problems of substandard housing interrelate closely with the issues of how individual housing choice and opportunity are allocated in our society. Immediate actions to ameliorate housing conditions constitute an important and vital holding action to preserve portions of the existing stock that we can ill afford to lose or replace. In the long run, however, these efforts are likely to prove inadequate and often futile until we have a better understanding of the factors that affect neighborhood attractiveness and stability and new ways of influencing residential settlement patterns can evolve and attain widespread acceptability.

Housing is perceived as a complex and insoluble issue because we have attempted to look at housing in counterproductive ways. The concept of filtration precludes recycling and has blinded us to the fact that for decades market processes have effectively been recycling much housing. Usually the better, more durable parts have been saved because of the working of such processes. Instead of trying to add brand new units in the heart of areas that have lost confidence or simply demolishing abandoned structures without wondering where the residents moved or what their job and income potential is, we must deepen our understanding of the processes that shape housing market dynamics so that humanistic policies can mold and channel those forces that encourage the recycling and preservation of housing.

A new role for the planner emerges, one less fixed on housing statistics and census data. Like the meteorologist, the new planner observes patterns of change, identifies areas where neighborhood confidence will wane for a time, and devises marketing programs to reshape the latent housing demand, channeling excess demand into neighborhoods with weak latent demand for housing. His tools will be new instruments for gauging neighborhood confidence and guiding and aiding troubled communities through the turmoil of change. Instead of simply counting dwelling units, conditions, and fix-up costs, he will view the urban areas as composed of households residing, going and coming by choice, and he will develop theories on what are now merely intuitions about the forces governing these movements. The new challenge is to devise incentives that can rearrange these movements into more productive patterns that raise neighborhood appeal.

Appendix A

Statistical Data on Boston's Population and Housing Stock

This Appendix provides the data base from which the Boston study was launched. This information is furnished here to enable readers in other cities to judge for themselves how relevant the Boston efforts are to their particular situation, as well as to permit those who wish to evaluate the Boston housing context themselves before accepting the conclusions and inferences presented in the various chapters of this book. The Appendix looks first at the people, then at their housing.

POPULATION TRENDS AND PROJECTIONS

An Overview

After two decades of decline, the population of Boston seems to have stabilized at about 645,000. Between 1950, the peak year of the city's population, and 1970, Boston lost approximately 160,000 persons, more than 100,000 during the first decade and over 50,000 during the sixties (see table A-1).

Boston's drop in population during the past two decades took place within the context of an expanding metropolitan area population although metropolitan growth lagged behind that of the nation as a whole and behind the growth levels of most metropolitan areas. Between 1950 and 1970, the population of the Boston SMSA (Standard Metropolitan Statistical Area) increased by 16 percent to almost 2,754,000 persons, while Boston's share of the SMSA's total population diminished from 34 percent to 23 percent.

However, it now appears that Boston's population decline has ended and that a modest increase in population has been occurring since

Table A-1. Population, City of Boston, 1950-70

Year	Population	Absolute Change	Percentage Change
1950	801,444	—	
1960	698,081	-103,363	-12.9%
1970	641,071	- 57,010	- 8.2%

Sources: 1950 and 1960 data from U.S. Bureau of the Census. 1970 data from 1970 Census of Population and Housing, First Count Summary Tape.

1970. Recently published estimates of 1972 population by the U.S. Bureau of the Census indicate that Suffolk County, encompassing Boston and three other small municipalities, has reversed its downward trend in population since 1970. The population of Suffolk County—739,500 in 1972—increased three-tenths of 1 percent during the 1970-72 period. This compares with an increase of eight-tenths of 1 percent in the population of the four suburban counties surrounding Suffolk (Essex, Middlesex, Norfolk and Plymouth). The recent Census Bureau figures point to a slowdown in population increases in the suburban counties of the Boston metropolitan area to half that of the 1950s and three-fourths that of the 1960s.[1]

Population projections to 1980 indicate that the recent slight rise in the population of the central city will continue during the remainder of the decade. Based on estimates of new construction, abandonments, and demolitions between 1970 and 1980, and an estimate of the 1980 population per dwelling unit by districts of the city, the population for Boston in 1980 has been projected at 662,618, an increase of about 22,000 or 3.3 percent over 1970 (see table A-2).

Although Boston has begun to experience a modest degree of population growth, the population of the SMSA will continue to increase at a much faster rate than that of the city. Projections for the SMSA to 1980 indicate a gain of approximately 250,000 people or 8.3 percent, more than double the city's projected rate of growth (see table A-3).

Trends in Household Size and Composition

Despite the 7 percent decline in Boston's population during the sixties, there was only a 3 percent decline (to 217,623) in the number of Boston's households.[2] Many families[3] migrating to the sub-

1. Population estimates for 1972 (July 1) from U.S. Bureau of the Census, *Current Population Reports*, Series P-25, No. 517, May 1974.
2. A household is defined here as one or more persons living in a single housing unit.
3. A family is defined as two or more persons living in the same household who are related by blood, marriage or adoption.

Table A-2. Estimated Population, City of Boston, 1980

District	Est. No. of Dwelling Units to be Demolished/Abandoned, 1970–80	Net Change in No. of Dwelling Units, 1970–80	Est. No. of Dwelling Units Through New Construction, 1970–80	Est. No. of Dwelling Units, 1980	Est. Population per Dwelling Unit, 1980	Est. Population, 1980
East Boston	1,181	+ 251	1,432	13,964	2.80	39,099
Charlestown	232	+ 960	1,192	6,105	2.95	18,010
South Boston	1,680	+ 2,496	4,176	16,722	2.60	43,477
North End	517	- 394	123	3,879	2.25	8,728
South Dorchester	751	+ 752	1,503	23,924	3.20	76,557
Back Bay-Beacon Hill	531	+ 1,389	1,920	18,285	1.70	31,085
Fenway-Kenmore	772	+ 2,587	3,359	16,589	2.50	41,473
Allston-Brighton	324	+ 1,708	2,032	27,052	2.50	67,630
Remaining Central	531	+ 6,606	7,137	10,440	1.83	19,105
South End	1,087	+ 1,104	2,191	11,861	2.30	27,280
Washington Park	7,054	- 5,810	1,244	19,175	2.90	55,608
Jamaica Plain	777	+ 633	1,410	17,191	2.75	47,275
North Dorchester	302	- 302	0	10,325	3.00	30,975
Mattapan	1,581	- 1,417	164	13,431	3.20	42,979
Roslindale	148	+ 102	250	12,303	3.10	38,139
West Roxbury	125	+ 1,985	2,110	12,659	3.10	39,243
Hyde Park	317	+ 121	438	11,236	3.20	35,955
Totals	17,910	+12,771	30,681	245,141	2.70 (average)	662,618

Sources: 1970 data from U.S. Bureau of the Census. 1980 estimates prepared by Research Department, Boston Redevelopment Authority.

Table A-3. Comparison of Populations, City of Boston and Boston SMSA, 1960-80

	Population, City of Boston	Percent Change over Prior Decade	Population, Boston SMSA	Percent Change over Prior Decade
1960	698,081		2,589,301	
1970	641,071	−8.2%	2,753,700	+6.3%
1980	662,618	+3.3%	3,000,000	+8.3%

Sources: 1960 and 1970 data from U.S. Bureau of the Census. 1980 estimates by Research Department, Boston Redevelopment Authority.

urbs or leaving the central city were replaced with households containing one or more unrelated individuals.[4] In fact, while the total number of families decreased by 14 percent, unrelated individuals increased by 27 percent, and the average number of persons per household decreased from 2.93 to 2.77. Some of the increased housing demand from the growing number of nonfamily groups has been met through conversions and the construction of smaller units. However, the shift in household type means that many larger family units are being occupied by unrelated individuals (often elderly people) or by groups of individuals sharing expenses (usually younger persons).

Trends in Age Groups

The above changes in household composition reflect very fundamental shifts in the age groups that make up Boston's population.

During the two decades between 1950 and 1970, Boston's age profile has been transformed from one roughly reflecting the national picture[5] to one which shows relatively larger proportions of young adults and elderly, but lower than typical percentages of children and persons of childrearing age. Table A-4 shows how Boston's age distribution compares in 1970 with that of the metropolitan area and the nation.

Perhaps the most dramatic development of the sixties was the sharp increase in the 20-24 year old group, which grew by 41 percent over that of the previous decade. This burst of population was not due to the maturation of the postwar babies. It was mainly attributable to the unprecedented expansion of educational facilities,

4. An unrelated individual is a person not living with relatives but living alone, in a household with persons not related to him or in group quarters (e.g., dormitories, nursing homes).
5. It is interesting to note that while Boston deviated from the national profile in the overrepresentation of young adults and the over-55 group, this situation also existed at the metropolitan level, although to a lesser degree.

Table A-4. Percentage Distribution of Population by Age Groups, City of Boston, Boston SMSA, and Nation, 1970

Age Group	Boston	SMSA	Nation
Under 5	7.8%	7.9%	8.4%
5-9	8.1	9.1	9.7
10-14	8.0	9.5	10.2
15-19	9.5	9.1	9.4
20-24	12.0	8.8	8.4
25-34	12.4	12.0	12.3
35-44	9.5	11.1	11.3
45-54	10.2	11.5	11.4
55-59	5.0	5.1	4.9
60-64	4.8	4.6	4.2
65-74	7.7	6.8	6.1
75 and over	5.0	4.6	3.8
Totals	100.0%	100.0%	100.0%

Source: U.S. Bureau of the Census.

the growth in service employment opportunities for younger adults and the generally strong attraction of the central city as a place of residence and work for younger persons. The impact, of course, was an increase in the already strong demand for housing in Boston by young, unrelated individuals, particularly in areas of the city close to university campuses, such as Allston-Brighton and Fenway-Kenmore. With the opening of the new University of Massachusetts campus early in 1974 and the anticipated doubling of its student enrollment (to 10,000) by 1980, additional growth in the number of young resident adults can be expected in the Boston neighborhoods of Dorchester and South Boston. The overall rate of growth in Boston's student population is likely to be tempered considerably, however, by the levelling off of enrollments in private college populations.

The population projections to 1980 assume that the upward trend in the 25-34 year old age bracket, which showed up during the early seventies, will continue. Much of the total population increase of 22,000 is expected to occur within this group, with some slight decreases in the 5-14 (-10,000) and 45-64 year olds (-4,000). The elderly population (over 65) is expected to remain unchanged by 1980 at just over the 80,000 level. (See table A-5 for a comparison of 1970 population by age group and by planning district.)

It is this growth of the 25-34 year old "young professionals" in Boston which brings added demands for new development and greater potential for an upgrading of the city's existing housing stock. Exactly who these people are and where they will choose to live are important questions for the future.

Table A-5.   Population for the City of Boston by Age Groups, 1970

Planning District	Total Population	Under 5	5-9	10-14	15-19	20-24	25-34
East Boston	38,873	3,182	3,264	3,439	3,274	3,283	4,363
Charlestown	15,353	1,258	1,429	1,581	1,544	1,320	1,686
South Boston	38,488	3,129	3,439	3,666	3,346	2,968	3,795
Central	19,334	876	840	803	1,196	2,553	3,039
Back Bay-Beacon Hill	27,538	520	301	229	3,572	7,944	5,405
South End	22,680	1,604	-,535	1,379	1,591	2,134	3,315
Fenway-Kenmore	32,965	573	314	245	8,394	11,396	3,685
Allston-Brighton	63,657	3,242	3,183	3,305	5,307	13,134	9,160
Jamaica Plain-Parker Hill	47,767	3,766	3,997	3,882	4,388	5,642	5,766
Washington Park-Model City	71,095	8,301	8,495	7,450	6,128	6,010	9,213
Washington Park	20,081	2,256	2,423	1,934	1,660	1,731	2,806
Campus High	1,749	150	226	158	135	114	176
Model City	49,265	5,895	5,846	5,308	4,333	4,165	6,231
Dorchester	152,529	15,122	15,725	14,980	13,116	12,249	17,978
Dorchester 1	32,665	3,274	3,544	3,449	2,983	2,609	3,636
Dorchester 2	74,415	7,056	7,377	7,251	6,480	5,828	8,479
Mattapan	45,449	4,792	4,804	4,280	3,653	3,812	5,863
Roslindale	39,558	3,115	3,306	3,631	3,246	3,010	4,379
West Roxbury	34,989	2,490	2,641	2,999	2,761	2,496	3,584
Hyde Park	34,977	2,743	3,219	3,443	3,037	2,819	3,842
Planning District Totals	639,803	49,921	51,688	51,032	60,900	76,958	79,210
Harbor Islands	1,241	1	14	16	160	145	143
Crews of Vessels	27			9			
City Totals	641,071	49,922	51,702	51,057	61,060	77,103	79,353

		35-44	45-54	55-59	60-64	65-74	75 & Over
East Boston	38,873	4,300	5,023	2,365	1,824	2,661	1,889
Charlestown	15,353	1,651	1,656	767	756	1,077	624
South Boston	38,488	3,747	4,642	2,264	2,019	3,140	2,316
Central	19,334	2,233	2,516	1,299	1,148	1,670	1,141
Back Bay-Beacon Hill	27,538	2,182	1,875	1,026	1,270	1,954	1,253
South End	22,680	2,553	2,734	1,186	1,293	2,088	1,251
Fenway-Kenmore	32,965	1,456	1,536	888	1,122	1,985	1,361
Allston-Brighton	63,657	4,870	5,421	3,075	3,278	5,994	3,684
Jamaica Plain-Parker Hill	47,767	4,170	4,529	2,302	2,425	4,047	2,834
Washington Park-Model City	71,095	7,414	6,766	2,636	2,195	3,682	2,800
Washington Park	20,081	2,199	1,831	693	564	1,117	814
Campus High	1,749	150	191	88	88	160	112
Model City	49,265	5,065	4,744	1,855	1,543	2,405	1,874
Dorchester	152,529	14,764	15,289	7,532	7,176	11,525	7,043
Dorchester 1	32,665	3,123	3,362	1,482	1,368	2,254	1,572
Dorchester 2	74,415	7,495	7,465	3,761	3,741	5,935	3,536
Mattapan	45,449	4,146	4,462	2,289	2,067	3,336	1,935
Roslindale	39,558	3,940	4,472	2,245	2,151	3,588	2,465
West Roxbury	34,989	3,508	4,265	2,366	2,263	3,561	2,055
Hyde Park	34,977	3,788	4,582	2,032	1,723	2,312	1,437
Planning District Totals	639,803	60,576	65,306	31,983	30,643	49,284	32,153
Harbor Islands	1,241	125	151	99	106	157	124
Crews of Vessels	27	18					
City Totals	641,071	60,719	65,457	32,082	30,749	49,441	32,277

Source: U.S. Census of Population and Housing, First Count Summary Tape.

Trends in Racial and Ethnic Composition

Boston's net decline of 20 percent in population between 1950 and 1970 obscured the significant increase in the city's racial minorities. While the total number of white persons decreased by 29 percent, the non-white population almost tripled, increasing from 43,000 persons or 5 percent of the population in 1950, to 116,000 persons or 18 percent of the population in 1970. This group is composed principally of black persons, whose population of about 105,000 in 1970 accounted for 16 percent of the city's total population. During these two decades, Boston absorbed 85 percent of the increase in the Boston area's black population; by 1970, with 23 percent of the SMSA population, Boston accounted for 82 percent of the area's black population.[6]

This absorption of so large an increase in black population has been accompanied in many areas by block busting, speculation, an increase in absentee-ownership, and intense racial conflict. Housing policies for the future must be directed at alleviating such problems and actions.

Another significant change in the composition of Boston's population during the sixties was the large increase in Spanish-Americans. In 1970 there were almost 18,000 such persons, comprising 2.8 percent of the city's population. Almost 40 percent of these were persons of Puerto Rican birth or parentage, a group which increased sevenfold during the decade. Boston now houses half of the metropolitan area's Spanish-Americans; 65 percent of these are Puerto Rican. Spanish-Americans are most heavily concentrated in the Model Cities area, Jamaica Plain, the South End and North Dorchester.

Racial Migration Trends

Black migration to the suburbs of central cities within Massachusetts has been relatively insignificant. Although the state's black

6. During the 1940s and 1950s, Boston's black population was largely confined to an area extending through the South End and Roxbury, each of which housed almost 45 percent of this group. During the decade of the fifties, the black population expanded numerically and followed a southward path toward Franklin Park. By 1960, the South End had lost black residents while the area that is now the Washington Park-Model Cities area (roughly coinciding with Roxbury) gained almost 22,000 blacks and accounted for 65 percent of the city's black population. During the sixties, black migration continued into Jamaica Plain and along the eastern side of Franklin Park extending into Mattapan. By 1970, Dorchester and Mattapan were housing 28 percent of the black population, totalling almost 30,000 persons. Nevertheless, Washington Park-Model Cities continued to be the area with the heaviest concentration of blacks: 75 percent of its population was black. Forty-one percent of the residents of Mattapan, 10 percent of Dorchester and 14 percent of Jamaica Plain were black in 1970 (see tables A-6 and A-7).

Table A–6. Non-White Population by Planning District, City of Boston, 1950, 1960, and 1970

Planning District	1950 Non-White Population	1960 Non-White Population	Change, 1950–60	1970 Non-White Population	Change, 1960–70
East Boston	75	71	– 4	442	+ 371
Charlestown	410	117	– 293	219	+ 102
South Boston	64	122	+ 58	673	+ 551
Central	1,778	2,039	+ 261	1,751	– 288
Back Bay, Beacon Hill	364	548	+ 184	1,067	+ 519
South End	18,486	14,585	– 3,901	11,949	– 2,636
Fenway-Kenmore	1,118	2,999	+ 1,881	2,986	– 13
Allston-Brighton	384	590	+ 206	2,646	+ 2,056
Jamaica Plain- Parker Hill	546	2,680	+ 2,134	7,628	+ 4,948
Washington Park- Model City	18,811	41,448	+22,637	54,128	+12,680
Washington Park	8,823	17,985	+ 9,162	18,576	+ 591
Campus High	5,145	3,063	– 2,082	1,444	– 1,619
Model Cities	4,843	20,400	+15,557	34,108	+13,708
Dorchester	213	1,445	+ 1,232	11,979	+10,534
Dorchester 1	77	1,090	+ 1,013	4,236	+ 3,146
Dorchester 2	136	355	+ 219	7,743	+ 7,388
Roslindale	148	399	+ 251	1,027	+ 628
West Roxbury	14	61	+ 47	229	+ 168
Hyde Park	53	108	+ 55	242	+ 134
Mattapan	165	473	+ 308	19,107	+18,634
Planning District Totals	42,629	67,685	+25,054	116,073	+48,388
Harbor Islands	115	198	+ 83	261	+ 63
Crews of Vessles	—	621	+ 621	—	– 621
City Totals	42,744	68,504	+25,730	116,334	+47,830

Sources: Data for 1950 and 1960 from U.S. Bureau of the Census; data for 1970 from U.S. Census of Population and Housing, First Count Summary Tape.

population increased by more than 57 percent from 1960 to 1970, more than four-fifths of the state's blacks in 1970 were still living in eight cities (the same pattern as in 1960): Boston, Brockton, Cambridge, Lynn, Medford, New Bedford, Springfield, and Worcester. Furthermore, within these cities, they tend to live in older, ghetto neighborhoods; they are not scattered among more affluent neighborhoods of such cities or in the suburban towns surrounding these cities. Within the Boston metropolitan area, 9 percent of all blacks live in the older cities, where black settlements have long existed—in Boston, Cambridge, Lynn, Medford, and Newton. Three out of every four municipalities in the Boston area have black populations which are less than 1 percent of the total population.

Table A-7. Percentage Distribution of Population by Race and Planning District, City of Boston, 1970

Planning District	Population	White	Black	American Indian	Other Specified Races*	Reported Other Races**
East Boston	38,873	98.8%	.8%	—	.1%	.1%
Charlestown	15,353	98.5	.5	.2%	.7	—
South Boston	38,488	98.2	1.0	.1	.4	.2
Central	19,334	90.8	1.4	.1	7.4	.2
Back Bay-Beacon Hill	27,538	96.1	2.2	.1	1.1	.4
South End	22,680	47.2	39.5	.2	12.2	.7
Fenway-Kenmore	32,965	90.9	6.1	.2	2.1	.6
Allston-Brighton	63,657	95.8	1.8	.1	2.0	.2
Jamaica Plain-Parker Hill	47,767	84.0	14.4	.1	.9	.5
Washington Park-Model City	71,095	23.8	74.7	.4	.3	.8
Washington Park	20,081	7.5	91.2	.4	.3	.5
Campus High	1,749	17.4	81.4	.7	—	.5
Model City	49,265	30.7	67.7	.4	.3	.9
Dorchester 1	32,665	87.0	11.8	.3	.3	.6
Dorchester 2	74,415	89.6	9.7	.1	.3	.2
Roslindale	39,558	97.4	1.9	—	.5	.1
West Roxbury	34,989	99.3	.2	—	.3	—
Hyde Park	34,977	99.3	.4	—	.3	—
Mattapan	45,449	57.9	41.0	.2	.4	.4
Planning District Totals	639,803	81.8	16.3	.2	1.3	.3
Harbor Islands	1,241	79.0	20.6	.2	.1	.1
Crew of Vessels	27	100.0	—	—	—	—
City Totals	641,071	81.9%	16.3%	.2%	1.3%	.3%

*Includes Chinese, Japanese, Filipino, Hawaiian, and Korean.
**Includes Asian Indians, Burmese, and other Asian nationalities.
Source: U.S. Census of Population and Housing for 1970, First Count Summary Tape.

Household Income

The real income of Boston's households rose by almost one-fourth during the decade of the sixties.[7] Not only are the incomes of resident Bostonians benefiting from the upgraded job market of the central city economy, but more middle- and upper-income households are also choosing city over suburban environments.

Despite these gains, however, the income discrepancy between Boston and most of its suburban neighbors, which was evident in 1960, has continued to widen.[8] There is an estimated $4,500 gap between the median family income of the central city ($9,100) and the estimated median family income for the remainder of the SMSA ($13,500). Moreover, there are significant differences in median family income as between the growing black and Spanish-speaking population in Boston and its white population. During the sixties this discrepancy worsened.[9] This trend runs contrary to the expectation that black incomes would approach the median as the number of black families increased and racial barriers declined.

Moreover, in 1970, some 32,000 households in Boston (covering almost 100,000 persons and accounting for 17 percent of the city's households) were reporting incomes which fell below the poverty level. With about one-fourth of the SMSA's households, Boston made up two-fifths of the area's households below the poverty level. Whereas 40 percent of the households in Boston earned $8,000 or less, the comparable percentage in the suburbs is only 22 percent (table A-8). It should be noted, however, that of the 23,200 unrelated poor persons in Boston between the ages of 14 and 24 in 1970, about 36 percent were college students not living in dormitories.[10]

The problem of poverty in Boston was much more serious among the elderly than the nonelderly population, and particularly among

7. Measured in constant dollars.
8. From 1960 to 1970, the median family income for the central city declined from 86 percent of the median family income for the entire SMSA to 80 percent of this same figure. While Boston's median family income increased by 22 percent, the increase for the SMSA as a whole was 30 percent (measured in constant dollars).
9. The median income of black families in the central city ($6,346 in 1970) declined from 74 percent of Boston's median family income in 1960 to 69 percent of Boston's median family income ($9,133) in 1970. The median family income of the city's Spanish-speaking population was even more depressed at 64 percent of Boston's median family income in 1970.
10. While many of the young adult population, and especially those who are students have incomes below the poverty level, this fact often reflects a life style which has been consciously chosen for a limited period of time. The pooling of resources by this group, although often out of necessity, as much as by choice, provides greater overall purchasing power in the housing market.

Table A-8. Distribution of Population by Income for 1970, City of Boston and Suburbs

Income Class	City of Boston		Suburbs (Boston SMSA excluding Boston)		Boston SMSA	
	Population	Percent of Total	Population*	Percent of Total	Population*	Percent of Total
Less than $ 5,000	139,101	21.7%	213,376	10.2%	352,477	12.9%
5,000 - 7,999	126,922	19.8	268,304	12.9	395,226	14.5
8,000 - 10,999	133,332	20.8	414,075	19.9	547,407	20.1
11,000 - 14,999	125,000	19.5	507,031	24.3	632,031	23.2
15,000 and over	116,666	18.2	682,380	32.7	799,046	29.3
Totals	641,021	100.0%	2,085,166	100.0%	2,726,187	100.0%

*Population figure understated by 27,464, not distributed by income class.

Source: Based on recalculation of 1970 census data by Research Department, Boston Redevelopment Authority.

elderly unrelated individuals, 39 percent of whom had incomes below the poverty line. In addition, poverty was more prevalent among certain racial and ethnic minorities. Twenty-eight percent of all black households and 32 percent of all Spanish-American households had incomes which fell below the poverty line.

Because of relatively low income, many of the city's households are spending a high proportion of their current resources on rent but are still unable to afford decent housing in the private market. An estimated 40 percent of all households who rent shelter in the city spent one-fourth or more of their income on rent in 1970.[11] In fact, the relatively high cost of housing in Boston, caused by higher than national average costs for property taxes, heating fuel and housing materials, ranks Boston as the most expensive large city to live within the continental United States.[12]

HOUSING TRENDS

Composition of the Housing Stock

The picture of Boston's housing stock that emerges from the 1970 Census is primarily one of relatively small, old structures. In 1970, there were 232,000 housing units in some 81,000 structures. Buildings with six or fewer units comprised 97 percent of all residential structures in the city, and contained two-thirds of all housing units. Over three-fourths of the city's dwellings were more than 30 years old in 1970, and a good proportion of these were built before the turn of the century.[13]

The median number of rooms per dwelling unit in Boston in 1970 was 5.2, which is large when compared with the average household size of 2.9. In many parts of the city—notably close-in sections like Allston-Brighton, Back Bay-Beacon Hill, and Charlestown—the demand for small units has led to conversions, both legally and illegally, of large units to smaller ones.[14] Despite the underutilization of larger units, often by elderly persons whose families have grown and left home, about 8 percent of Boston's occupied units

11. From table A-2, U.S. Bureau of the Census, Census of Population and Housing: 1970, *Census Tracts*, Final Report PH (c)(1)-29, Boston, Mass., SMSA.
12. U.S. Department of Labor, Bureau of Labor Statistics, Table 1. "Annual Costs of a Lower Budget for a 4-Person Family" (Autumn, 1973).
13. As would be expected, the housing stock in Boston is older than that of its neighbors in the SMSA. In 1970, according to the Census, with 26 percent of the area's units, Boston accounted for 32 percent of those built before 1940, but only 14 percent of those built in 1969.
14. The financial advantages of conversions to investors (two small units are more profitable than one large unit) had led, in areas of rising demand by young persons, to the displacement of renting families.

were classified as overcrowded in 1970.[15] Compared with overcrowding in the Boston SMSA, in central cities as a whole and in the nation as a whole, Boston's rate of overcrowding (7.6 percent) is not serious.[16]

Changes and Additions to the Housing Stock

During the decade of the sixties, the city experienced a net *decrease* of almost 6,400 units, or 2.7 percent in its housing stock. This change was the result of new construction amounting to slightly more than 20,000 units entirely offset by the demolition and changed uses for almost 27,000 residential units (over 11 percent of the stock). Most of the demolished housing was located in urban renewal areas.[17] It is estimated that demolition activity in the sixties was split between brick masonry structures and wood-frame buildings, with about two-thirds being wood.

Of the 20,000 housing units built, one-quarter were low- and moderate-rental units (mainly federally-subsidized), the other three-quarters serving households in the middle- and upper-income price range. As already mentioned, most of this construction was for high density apartments. New housing was built throughout the city, but certain outlying districts—West Roxbury, Hyde Park, Allston-Brighton, and South Dorchester, in particular—experienced the greatest growth in private apartment house development and the "inner city" neighborhoods received the largest percentage of subsidized housing. In addition, during the early part of the sixties, some single-family wood frame homes were built in the more suburban sections of the city such as West Roxbury, Hyde Park, Roslindale, and the Moss Hill section of Jamaica Plain.

New construction in the city during the first three years of the seventies has been at about the same rate as in the sixties, approximately 2,000 units per year. Moreover, a large backlog of new construction can be identified by looking at proposed housing developments. Practically all of these units will be high density apartments. The large majority, however, are in the tentative stages (about two-thirds). Given the uncertainties regarding the allocation of federal housing subsidies, pressures for limiting growth, requirements for environmental impact controls, fears and cautions

15. An overcrowded unit is defined here as one which houses 1.01 or more persons per room.

16. For all central cities in the nation, the overcrowding rate in 1970 was 8.5 percent; the Boston SMSA 1970 overcrowding rate was 5.7 percent; for all SMSAs in the nation, it was 7.8 percent.

17. There also has been a loss during the early seventies of several thousand dwelling units, some of which have been demolished due to abandonment.

concerning rent control, a depressed housing market, dwindling mortgage loans, high interest rates, etc., the future of this potential development is in doubt without firm, large-scale inputs of public subsidy and commitment.

It is also important to note that there has been a rather dramatic shift in the financing and beneficiaries of new construction between the sixties and the early seventies. Whereas only one-fourth of new construction in the sixties received public subsidies, three-fourths of the units constructed or under construction in the seventies have received such public assistance. Furthermore, the Massachusetts Housing Finance Agency (MHFA), which recently began to play an increasingly important role in financing housing within the central city, is now in difficulties attempting to avoid default on its own outstanding bonds.

This shift to subsidized private housing construction, added to Boston's traditional commitment to conventional public housing, dramatizes the fact that Boston serves as the principal location for subsidized and public housing in the SMSA. The city has less than one-fourth of the metropolitan area's population, but over half the area's subsidized private and/or public housing. As of the end of 1973 there were some 71,000 units of subsidized private and public housing in the metropolitan area, either completed or under construction, 38,000 of them in Boston; 16 percent of the housing stock in the city is publicly-assisted as compared with only 4 percent of the housing stock in the metropolitan area exclusive of Boston.[18]

There has also been a shift in the location of new residential construction in Boston since the 1960s. During the 1960s, new housing was built throughout the entire city. During the first three years of the seventies there has been a residential development shift to the downtown, particularly of housing for middle- and upper-income groups, with two-thirds of new private construction located in the core area of Boston. This compares to only 20 percent in the core area during the sixties. There has also been a shift in the scale of development, with projects of fifty units or more dominating residential construction in the city.

Such shifts indicate that outside the downtown area, the private

18. Metropolitan Area Planning Council, *Subsidized Housing in the Boston Region as of December 21, 1973* (Boston, Mass., 1974). The city's proportions of the metropolitan area's total number of completed housing units found in the several federally and state assisted housing programs are as follows: family public housing, 60 percent; elderly public housing, 20 percent; leased public housing, 55 percent; section 221(d)(3) and 236 subsidized housing, 78 percent; Massachusetts Housing Finance Agency assisted units, 56 percent.

financing of new multifamily housing construction in the city has practically ceased. A number of factors have contributed to this: rising costs of construction and maintenance, lack of developable land, the dependence on MHFA financing and suburban location as an appealing alternative, and no-growth and environmental concerns. With the federal moratorium on subsidized housing in effect since January 1973, and not really eased by the new federal Section 8 programs, any major new residential building in Boston in the short run, other than in the downtown area (unless other areas in the city become particularly attractive), is doubtful until there is clarification concerning allocation of the 400,000 units authorized for lower income housing assistance under provisions of the 1974 Housing and Community Development Act.[19] Most of the city's housing needs in the near future are not likely to be met through new housing construction; and it is therefore imperative to focus on preserving the existing housing stock.

Regardless of what happens concerning new construction, continued pressure for conversions of older retail, warehouses or commercial structures to residential purposes is anticipated because of growing market demand. Preliminary estimates indicate that as many as 3,600 dwelling units are planned in conversions in the downtown area from nonresidential uses. A corollary trend observable in the city is the conversion of rental units to condominium ownership. Although only some 1,500 condominiums have or are in the process of being converted from existing rental units in the city, as the idea catches on in New England and as condominiums are used as an escape from rent control, it is anticipated that the pressure for conversion to condominium ownership will grow. Such pressures have both positive and negative aspects: positive because of the potential for upgrading the city's housing; negative because of the upheaval that may result for existing tenants if care and precautions are not taken.

Condition of the Housing Stock[20]

Most of Boston's housing stock is in good condition. Thirty percent meets existing code standards; another 40 percent is basically

19. In its Housing Assistance Plan, submitted to the Department of Housing and Urban Development in 1975, Boston committed most of its allocation to MHFA to facilitate development. Considering the long lead time required for development as well as MHFA's financial difficulties in "rolling over" its current moral obligation bonds, protracted delays are expected even though many designs are on the drawing boards.

20. Data from field survey conducted in 1973 by Housing Inspection Department, City of Boston. See Chapter 3 for a further description of the methodology and subsequent application of the data.

in good condition, requiring only modest fix-up to be brought up to code standards. However, one-fourth of the stock requires considerable fix-up, an additional 4 percent need gut rehabilitation and 1 percent should be demolished.

This summary of housing conditions is far more realistic than conclusions that might be drawn from an analysis based on the trend in the total number of dwelling units categorized by the U.S. Bureau of the Census as "dilapidated." In fact, according to the Census, during the 1960s the number of dilapidated units decreased from 9,200 (3.9 percent of the city's total) to 6,600 (2.8 percent of the city's total).[21] If the rate of change of the 1960s continued during the next decade, Boston's housing stock would contain few if any dilapidated housing.

It should be noted, however, that the several forces which generated the significant improvement in housing conditions during the 1960s are not likely to leave equally significant imprints on the city's housing stock. During the 1960s over 8,000 dwelling units located in four urban renewal project areas of Boston were rehabilitated (4,000 in Roxbury's Washington Park, 2,000 in the South End, 1,000 in Charlestown, and 1,000 in the Fenway area), most of them with the assistance of federal loans and grants. Another 1,000 housing units were similarly rehabilitated (in Dorchester and Jamaica Plain) through the federally-aided Community Improvement Program. Equally significant, moreover, was the demolition through urban renewal during the 1960s of over 15,000 housing units, most of which have been or will have been replaced by new federally-subsidized housing construction of one kind or another. The subsidy opportunities under which most of the subsidized new construction and rehabilitation was undertaken in the 1960s and early 1970s have been either terminated or drastically curtailed. Community development revenue sharing and housing assistance available under the 1974 Housing and Community Development Act will not give Boston during the 1970s the scale of resources which would enable the city to replicate the improvement in housing conditions carried out during the prior decade.

The highest requirements for fix-up are found in the inner-city area of Washington Park-Model Cities, in the transitional areas of western Dorchester and the northern sector of Jamaica Plain, in the older, ethnic areas of South and East Boston, and in the South

21. U.S. Bureau of the Census, *Components of Inventory Change*, May 1973, HC(4)-3. Since the data in this report was based on a sample of some 14,000 housing units located "in clusters or land area segments representative of the SMSA," it undoubtedly understates the proportion of the city's housing stock requiring rehabilitation.

Cove. Areas with high fix-up needs roughly coincide with areas where incomes and effective housing demand are low.

Despite the fact that less than one-third of Boston's stock is in full compliance with the housing code, the market strength for housing throughout most of the city remains at least adequate if not strong, and it is estimated that almost 80 percent of the substandard housing stock has the potential of being upgraded privately, public actions being used as leverage to help stimulate private investment. Upgrading of the remaining 20 percent, however, can only occur with heavy government assistance.

Current housing conditions provide only a static measure of the soundness of the housing stock. Other characteristics of the housing market itself—tenure, turnover, vacancies, rents, and values—are additional useful indicators for measuring the future health of the stock.

Ownership Patterns and Trends

Traditionally, older sections in Boston's neighborhoods have been kept in good condition because their owner-residents have maintained them. Boston's degree of owner-occupancy is lower than that of the SMSA, however, where 53 percent of all units are owner-occupied. Only 27 percent of all housing *units* were owner-occupied in 1970, but approximately 71 percent of all residential *structures* fell into this category.[22] Among smaller structures containing four or fewer units, the degree of owner occupancy was 77 percent. (See table A-9 for differences in owner-occupancy by district.)

The ratio of owner-occupancy did not change for the city's housing stock as a whole during the 1960s, although there were considerable fluctuations by area. Decreases in owner-occupancy of one- to four-unit structures occurred in parts of Fenway-Kenmore, Allston-Brighton, the South End, Washington Park-Model Cities, western Dorchester, East Boston, and Charleston. This downward trend is also showing up in Jamaica Plain and Mission Hill. Although owner-occupancy of one- to four-unit structures in Boston increased during the decade, from 64 percent to 77 percent of the total, this was largely due to the demolition of approximately 7,500 primarily absentee-owned, one- to four-unit structures, rather than any significant trends towards increased resident ownership in the turnover of the housing stock.

The tradition of resident ownership is decidedly threatened in areas like Jamaica Plain and Allston-Brighton, where a high propor-

22. The large difference between the percentage of owner-occupied units and structures is in part accounted for by the large number of triple-decker and two-family units in the city.

Table A-9. Housing Units by Occupancy Status and Planning District, City of Boston, 1970

Planning District	Total Housing Units	Occupied Units	Total Owner- Occ. (Percent Occ. Units)		Total Renter Occ. (Percent Occ. Units)	
East Boston	13,709	12,843	3,940	(30.7%)	8,903	(69.3%)
Charlestown	5,119	4,815	1,559	(32.4)	3,256	(67.6)
South Boston	14,259	13,375	3,459	(25.9)	9,916	(74.1)
Central	9,664	8,727	779	(8.9)	7,948	(91.1)
Back Bay- Beacon Hill	15,622	14,462	920	(6.4)	13,542	(93.6)
South End	10,719	8,968	1,013	(11.3)	7,955	(88.7)
Fenway-Kenmore	13,243	12,288	260	(2.1)	12,028	(97.9)
Allston-Brighton	25,324	24,540	4,732	(19.3)	19,808	(80.7)
Jamaica Plain- Parker Hill	17,093	15,894	3,582	(22.5)	12,312	(77.5)
Washington Park- Model City	24,958	22,002	4,606	(20.9)	17,396	(79.1)
Washington Park	6,957	6,481	1,132	(11.5)	5,349	(82.5)
Campus High	826	591	89	(15.1)	502	(84.9)
Model City	17,175	14,930	3,385	(22.7)	11,545	(77.3)
Dorchester	33,727	32,099	10,981	(34.2)	21,118	(65.8)
Dorchester 1	10,466	9,854	2,488	(25.2)	7,366	(74.8)
Dorchester 2	23,261	22,245	8,493	(38.2)	13,752	(61.8)
Roslindale	12,253	11,990	5,399	(45.0)	6,591	(55.0)
West Roxbury	11,026	10,906	7,316	(67.1)	3,590	(32.9)
Hyde Park	10,735	10,480	6,120	(58.4)	4,360	(41.6)
Mattapan	14,950	14,046	4,512	(32.1)	9,534	(67.9)
Planning District Totals	232,401	217,435	59,178	(27.2)	158,257	(72.8)
Harbor Islands	38	38	—		38	
Crews of Vessels	9	5	5		—	
City Totals	232,448	217,478	59,183	(27.2%)	158,295	(72.8%)

Source: U.S. Census of Population and Housing, 1970, First Count Summary Tape.

tion of owners in 1970 were over 62 years old. In fact, in 1970 the elderly owned 28 percent of all one- to four-unit structures in Boston.[23] Since these structures tended to be larger (containing more units on the average than those owned by nonelderly persons), they accounted for a greater share of all units located in owner-occupied buildings. Many of these elderly owners now live alone on fixed incomes in larger housing than they really require, and it is questionable how well they themselves are able to care for their homes.

On the whole, residential owners in the central city had higher

23. Elderly ownership is quite high in Boston compared to that in the SMSA, where only 20 percent of all owners are elderly.

incomes than their renter counterparts, with a median income of $10,500 as compared to $6,100 for the latter group. They also tended to have larger households on the average than renters (median of 3.1 persons, as compared with 2.0). Despite the large number of elderly, the majority of homeowners in 1970 consisted of nonelderly families with both husband and wife present.

Black households comprised 15 percent of the city's households in 1970 but made up only 9 percent of the city's homeowners. They tended to own structures which were older (93 percent of their homes were built before 1949, as opposed to 87 percent for the city's owner-occupants at large) and larger (75 percent owned structures with two or more units, as compared with 52 percent of the city's owner-occupants at large).

Black owners were also younger (only 12 percent were elderly), had lower incomes (with a 1969 median of $8,800) and had purchased their homes relatively recently (19 percent had moved in between 1969 and March 1970, compared to 6.6 percent of the city's owner-occupants at large).

Given the relative scarcity of large-scale owners in Boston, what is happening to those who are here? Except for sponsors of federally-subsidized housing (who are locked into ownership through federal tax laws),[24] and owners of sizable luxury developments, a number of major landlords seem to be getting out of the business. This applies both to those who can aptly be described as slumlords because their buildings are decaying in inner city areas and to those whose holdings are in more marginal areas of Boston. Several of them have blamed both economics and politics for increasing the difficulty of managing housing in Boston to the point that it is no longer a profitable business. Economics is blamed for rising prices of housing services, utilities, and interest rates, without a corresponding rise in tenants' incomes to support the rents required to meet increased expenses. Politics is blamed for rent control, with public authority over rent increases and tenant evictions, which, according to some owners, has gone too far in supporting tenants' rights against landlords' rights.

If large owners *are* selling off their property, the interesting question for housing policy is: who is buying the housing? The answer

24. Owners of Section 221(d)(3) and Section 236 developments are in a special situation. Perhaps half of these developments in Boston are no longer meeting their debt service obligations, but the federal government has ceased attempting to foreclose. Apparently HUD is attempting to devise another way to meet the higher than anticipated costs of housing low and moderate income households in such developments.

is not yet clear. While in one or two cases one large owner has bought out another, this is an exceptional occurrence. In general, large holdings appear to be purchased piecemeal by all types of small owners. Their ability to maintain, much less upgrade, the housing varies considerably. One shrewd owner characterized the purchasers of his former possessions as unsuspecting amateurs on whom he unloaded unsalvageable buildings. It does seem that less competent "second stringers" are the main buyers of investor-owned multifamily housing.[25]

Housing Turnover

Gross data on population and household changes fail to capture the more microscopic movement of individual households which forms the fabric of the housing market. As table A-10 indicates, almost one-quarter of all households in Boston had lived in their units for less than fifteen months at the time of the 1970 Census, and more than half had been in their homes for five years or less. In comparison with 1960, Boston's 1970 housing stock was inhabited by a greater proportion of newcomers and a smaller proportion of old-timers who had occupied their units for more than twenty years. In addition, the tenure of households in Boston in 1970 was shorter than that of other households in the SMSA.

As might be expected, the average tenure was shorter among renters than among owners. Among owners, lower-income households in 1970 were far more stable residentially than higher-income households, doubtlessly due to the relatively high proportion of elderly in the former group. Among renters, however, higher incomes meant somewhat more stability.

The black population in 1970 was considerably more mobile than the city's households at large. This was mainly attributable to the opening of additional residential neighborhoods to blacks toward the end of the sixties, to the rapid exodus of white families from these areas and to the greater tendency of black families to move rather frequently. One-third of all black households in 1970 had moved into their dwellings between 1969 and March 1970, and only 13 percent had occupied the same dwelling for more than ten years.

Turnover has been highest in areas containing a high proportion of renters (especially where renters are young) and in those areas which have recently undergone racial transition.

25. In December 1975, the Boston Redevelopment Authority Research Department initiated a comprehensive study of multifamily investor-owned properties.

Table A-10. Housing Turnover in City of Boston and Boston SMSA, 1960 and 1970

| | Households in 1970 | | |
| | Boston | | SMSA |
Year Moved In	*Number*	*Percent*	*Percent*
1969–March 1970	53,988	24.8%	18.0%
1968	24,823	11.4	9.7
1967	17,213	7.9	7.0
1965–1966	25,410	11.7	11.2
1960–1964	32,301	14.8	16.5
1950–1959	31,640	14.5	20.0
1949 or earlier	32,243	14.8	17.5
Total	217,618	100.0%	100.0%
	Households in 1960		
1958–March 1960	69,943	31.1%	26.6%
1954–1957	58,434	26.0	26.0
1940–1953	60,605	27.0	30.7
1939 or earlier	35,705	15.9	17.0
Total	224,687	100.0%	100.0%

Sources: U.S. Bureau of the Census.

Housing Vacancies and Abandonment

In April 1973, over 6,500 dwelling units, or 3.5 percent of the city's housing stock, were vacant. This compares with the SMSA figure of over 10,500 units, or 2.5 percent. Since the data base for these rates excludes single-family structures, and it can be assumed that single-family vacancies are negligible, these ratios are undoubtedly overstated. (Housing vacancy data for city of Boston, local postal zones of Boston and Boston area are shown in table A-11.) These recent vacancy rates reflect not only a tightening of the housing market in the Boston area, including the central city, but a narrowing of the vacancy rate gap during the past few years as between Boston and the SMSA. In 1970 data from the U.S. Bureau of the Census showed Boston with a vacancy rate of 6.5 percent as compared with 3.5 percent for the entire SMSA.

Vacant units in Boston are found disproportionately in larger buildings containing five or more dwellings, but they tend to carry rentals below the city median. High vacancy rates may, with some caution, be used as a proxy for lack of housing demand, and often coincide with declining housing values.

The abandonment of property by owners is the most extreme condition of vacancy and may be considered the ultimate sign of lack

Table A-11. Housing Vacancy Rates for April 1973 in City of Boston and Boston Area

Post Office District	Total No. of Housing Units in Survey	Existing Buildings	New (Not Occupied)	Total	Housing Vacancy Rate
		No. of Vacant Units			
Boston Area	426,283	8,879	1,684	10,563	2.5%
Boston (city)	188,009	5,605	969	6,574	3.5%
Brighton	23,913	513	4	517	2.2%
Allston 02134	8,283	262	0	262	3.2%
Brighton 02135	13,964	221	0	221	1.6%
Chestnut Hill 02167	1,666	30	4	34	2.0%
Dorchester	33,532	1,049	2	1,051	2.7%
Fields Corner 02122	5,540	166	0	166	3.0%
Codman Sq. 02124	12,895	758	0	758	5.9%
Mattapan 02126	6,780	49	2	51	0.8%
Uphams Corner 02125	13,317	76	0	76	0.6%
East Boston 02128	12,911	119	6	125	1.0%
South Boston 02127	12,283	183	1	184	1.5%
Charlestown 02129	8,364	132	0	132	1.6%
Jamaica Plain 02130	11,537	462	2	464	4.0%
Roslindale 02131	7,260	66	0	66	0.9%
West Roxbury 02132	2,975	15	5	20	0.7%
Hyde Park 02136	961	53	0	53	5.5%
Roxbury-South End	34,918	1,720	164	1,884	5.4%
Cathedral 02116	6,781	297	149	466	6.6%
Grove Hall 02121	11,006	403	0	403	3.7%
Roxbury 02119	17,131	1,020	15	1,035	6.0%
Back Bay 02115, 6, 7 02215	25,228	1,095	565	1,660	6.6%
Gov't Center-Central	9,127	198	220	418	4.6%

Note: The Postal Vacancy Survey is conducted periodically by local post offices in cooperation with the U.S. Department of Housing and Urban Development (HUD). The apartment vacancy rate reflects vacancies in units on any postal delivery stop where more than one mail delivery is possible. Single-family homes (owner or renter-occupied) are not included. Boarded-up residences or apartments not intended for occupancy are not included.

of demand. During the year ending October 1972, an estimated 970 residential structures (1 percent of the city's structures containing some 3,000 dwelling units) were, from all appearances, abandoned, although some of these may have since been restored. A disproportionately large share of these structures were owned by absentee-landlords and were located in Washington Park-Model Cities and West Dorchester. Structures with three and four units appear to be most vulnerable to problems which eventually lead to abandonment.[26]

Value of the Housing Stock

Trends in value of the housing stock are useful rough measures of market viability. Over the past two and a half decades, the value of one- to four-unit residential structures in Boston has been growing steadily though slowly.[27] A typical property located in a stable neighborhood of the city and purchased for $10,000 in 1946 would sell for $19,999 in 1960 ($10,880, controlling for inflation) and $37,500 in 1972 ($14,540, controlling for inflation).

For apartment house structures, preliminary indications are that value increases ceased around 1970. There have been relatively few multifamily structures sold recently rendering actual market value data difficult to obtain, but the BRA Research Department estimates that current high interest rates compound with the effects of rent control and the uncertainties regarding property tax revaluations, have reduced the current value of investor-owned stock by 30 percent over 1967.[28]

Residential property values in Boston are lower than in the SMSA as a whole. Boston's median reported value of a single-family house in 1970 was $19,600, compared with the SMSA median of $23,900. Moreover, while the value of single-family houses increased during the 1960s by 12 percent in the SMSA, in Boston it increased by only 8 percent.[29] Values are the highest by far in areas which have ex-

26. See Francine Price, "Abandonment in Boston: The Dimensions of the Problem," Boston Redevelopment Authority Research Department, April 1973.

27. See John Avault and Robert F. Engle, "Residential Property Market Values in Boston," Boston Redevelopment Authority Research Department, 1973. In this study, price indexes for Boston at large and for individual districts were constructed on the basis of the sale prices of properties which had changed hands more than once between 1946 and 1972. These price indexes have since been adjusted to account for inflation.

28. See Edward Blaine, "Erosion of Real Property Values in Multi-Family Real Estate," Boston Redevleopment Authority Research Department, December 1975.

29. Unfortunately, a price index similar to the one constructed to compare values of residential properties in Boston is not available for the SMSA at large. Boston-SMSA comparisons are based on U.S. Census data, controlled for the effects of inflation.

perienced more recent increases in value: Back Bay-Beacon Hill and Central Boston. Property values are still substantially below the city median in the older neighborhoods: South Boston, Charlestown, and East Boston, despite their recent gains in market values, and in Washington Park-Model Cities and North Dorchester, where values have been falling (see table A-12).

Changes in values have not been equally distributed throughout the city, however. Between 1960 and 1970, for example, the greatest gains in residential property market prices were occurring in Charlestown (increase of over 25 percent), the South End (24 percent) undergoing neighborhood upgrading as a result of urban renewal activities. Substantial gains were also evident in East Boston (over 10 percent), South Boston (8.5 percent), Back Bay-Beacon Hill (almost 13 percent), and Allston-Brighton (over 7 percent).[30] By and large these gains are attributable to demand for 1–4 unit structures generated by a proximity to the downtown, often compounded by increased demand by young adults. Declines in value after adjusting for inflation were occurring in the inner city area of Washington Park-Model Cities, and in the transitional neighborhoods of Dorchester and Mattapan-Franklin and probably in the majority of investor-owned, multi-unit structures.

Rents

Boston's increase of 23 percent in contract rent during the 1960s (measured in constant dollars) lagged only slightly behind the SMSAs increase of 26 percent, and the increases in gross rent were approximately equal.

Rents are relatively low in the older ethnic neighborhoods, as well as in inner-city and racially-transitional neighborhoods. They are highest in areas undergoing strong demand—Back Bay-Beacon Hill, Fenway-Kenmore, and Allston-Brighton—as well as in the more suburban sections of the city (see table A-13).

Since rents tend to respond quickly to rising demand, it is not surprising that rents were simultaneously showing substantial increases in Charlestown, Central Boston, the South End, South Boston and Allston-Brighton. They were increasing rapidly in the Mission Hill, Forest Hills and Hyde Square sections of Jamaica Plain, the Savin Hill section of Dorchester and, perhaps surprisingly, in Mattapan.

30. Avault and Engle, "Residential Property Market Values in Boston," Boston Redevelopment Authority, Research Department, 1973, especially p. 19–23. This research was based on owner's estimates of what price their homes would bring on the market. Biases in respondents' estimates of house values are acknowledged: high priced houses may have been underestimated to a greater degree in fear of reassessment; houses in deteriorating areas may not even have had a potential market.

Table A–12. Distribution of Value* of Owner-Occupied Single-Family Homes, City of Boston, 1970

Planning District	Total No. of Owner Occup. Units**	Less Than $5,000	$5,000 to 9,999	$10,000 to 14,999	$15,000 to 19,999	$20,000 to 24,999	$25,000 to 34,999	$35,000 to 49,000	$50,000 or More	Median
East Boston	900	5.2%	20.2%	26.0%	22.5%	12.3%	9.8%	3.2%	.8%	$14,721
Charlestown	826	8.2	29.3	28.8	22.2	6.9	3.3	.7	.6	12,163
South Boston	1,326	14.3	34.0	26.6	18.0	5.0	1.4	.5	.2	10,326
Central	65	1.5	16.9	9.2	7.7	7.7	15.4	23.1	18.5	29,500
Back Bay-Beacon Hill	343	.3	.6	.9	.9	3.8	5.8	10.8	76.9	67,519
South End	397	3.5	10.6	21.9	16.9	11.8	15.9	11.8	7.6	19,141
Fenway-Kenmore	55	1.8	12.7	12.7	23.7	20.0	18.2	10.9	—	19,807
Allston-Brighton	1,605	1.1	3.8	11.9	26.6	30.6	21.2	4.1	.7	21,082
Jamaica Plain-Parker Hill	1,486	.9	8.4	16.1	17.8	14.5	23.3	16.1	2.9	22,338
Washington Park-Model City	1,128	9.7	34.2	29.7	19.6	5.1	1.1	.5	.1	11,015
Washington Park	218	5.1	22.9	36.7	24.3	8.7	2.3	—	—	12,999
Campus High	50	22.0	30.0	28.0	10.0	6.0	2.0	2.0	—	9,666
Model City	860	10.2	37.3	28.0	19.0	4.1	.7	.6	.1	10,436
Dorchester	5,889	1.1	6.9	22.7	36.0	24.2	8.1	.9	.1	17,672
Dorchester 1	651	3.4	16.0	36.6	31.6	8.1	3.7	.5	.1	14,190
Dorchester 2	3,394	1.0	6.3	23.0	37.7	23.7	7.3	.9	.1	17,611
Mattapan	1,844	.5	4.8	17.4	34.4	30.6	11.1	1.1	.1	18,966
Roslindale	3,089	.4	1.7	9.9	39.0	34.4	13.0	1.3	.3	19,868
West Roxbury	6,011	.1	1.3	5.0	20.3	35.7	32.7	4.0	.9	23,253
Hyde Park	4,350	.4	1.9	10.5	33.4	36.7	15.6	1.4	.1	20,520
Totals	27,470	2.1%	7.8%	14.9%	27.7%	26.6%	16.2%	3.1%	1.6%	$19,600

*Based upon the respondent's estimate of how much the property would sell for on the current market.

**Value is not ascertained for owner-occupied and vacant available for sale units which are in multi-unit structures, trailers, rural units on farms or places of ten or more acres, or on properties part of which is used as a business.

Source: U.S. Census of Population and Housing, First Count Summary Tape.

Table A-13.   Monthly Contract Rent for Occupied Rental Housing Units in City of Boston, 1970

Planning District	Total Renter Occupied Units With Cash Rent*	Less Than $40	$40 to $59	$60 to $79	$80 to $99	$100 to $119	$120 to $149	$150 to $199	$200 to $299	$300 or More	Median
East Boston	8,697	8.3%	28.9%	34.3%	14.4%	7.1%	5.3%	1.5%	.1%	.1%	$ 67
Charlestown	3,173	3.7	22.6	38.7	21.3	8.1	3.7	1.4	.5	—	72
South Boston	9,763	4.7	23.7	36.4	19.8	7.3	5.0	2.9	.2	—	71
Central	7,861	5.6	17.0	18.4	9.0	8.0	8.1	12.3	14.1	7.5	99
Back Bay-Beacon Hill	13,338	.6	1.8	6.6	7.9	8.4	17.5	28.0	19.4	9.8	163
South End	7,849	3.9	17.3	34.3	19.6	12.0	8.1	2.7	1.8	.3	76
Fenway-Kenmore	11,801	.5	2.3	9.3	18.5	20.3	23.8	19.5	4.8	1.0	118
Allston-Brighton	19,591	.3	3.2	5.7	10.5	16.2	27.9	24.5	10.6	1.1	135
Jamaica Plain-Parker Hill	12,161	1.0	9.1	26.1	22.8	12.6	11.9	9.5	6.0	1.0	92
Washington Park-Model City	17,140	1.5	9.6	27.5	25.6	22.1	12.3	1.3	.1	—	88
Washington Park	5,229	.4	6.3	17.7	21.9	31.1	20.3	2.1	.2	—	102
Campus High	493	7.1	34.5	43.8	10.4	2.2	1.6	.4	—	—	64
Model City	11,418	1.8	10.0	31.3	28.0	18.8	9.0	1.0	.1	—	85
Dorchester	30,292	.7	4.9	22.0	34.6	19.3	10.9	6.9	.7	—	92
Dorchester 1	7,298	1.1	8.3	34.9	35.7	11.4	5.0	3.5	.1	—	83
Dorchester 2	13,570	.8	4.2	19.5	39.1	20.1	10.6	5.5	.2	—	92
Mattapan	9,424	.4	3.0	15.8	27.3	24.1	15.7	11.7	2.0	—	103
Roslindale	6,421	.7	4.8	14.5	24.8	22.8	20.6	11.1	.7	—	104
West Roxbury	3,446	1.0	.7	3.0	9.7	15.2	35.3	28.6	6.4	.1	137
Hyde Park	4,239	1.2	4.9	13.0	23.4	19.2	14.3	20.9	3.1	—	107
Totals	155,772	1.9%	9.1%	20.0%	20.5%	15.3%	14.7%	11.9%	5.1%	1.5%	$ 98

*Figures exclude 2,069 rental housing units with no cash rent.
Source: U.S. Census of Population and Housing, 1970, First Count Summary Tape.

SYNTHESIS OF POPULATION AND
HOUSING DATA

While population and housing market trends have been discussed separately, they have a strong influence on each other. The significant demographic changes described earlier—the loss of middle-income families and the gain in the 20 to 24 age group, blacks, and more recently of 25 to 34 year old "young professionals"—have affected market strength and introduced new housing demand groups with purchasing power which was both higher and lower than that of former residents. Thus, it is important at this point to underscore this relationship between supply and demand, particularly as it relates to Boston's various neighborhoods.

During the 1950s and 1960s, the greatest population losses occurred in two types of neighborhoods: (1) in inner-city areas when there was abandonment and also demolition for urban renewal. (This type of loss is best typified by the South End, although a turnabout in the area began to occur in the late 1960)s. (2) in the older, ethnic areas—such as East Boston, Charlestown, South Boston, and the North End—where rising incomes and an aging housing stock both contributed to the loss of families to suburbia.

Meanwhile, other areas—notably North Dorchester and Mattapan, where units are large and relatively low in cost—remained fairly unchanged until the late 1960s, at which time there was widespread population movement associated with racial transition.

Similarly, there were few major changes in Back Bay-Beacon Hill, Fenway-Kenmore, and Allston-Brighton until the mid-1960s when attractive location and rentals began to draw a growing young adult population (mainly college students), ultimately resulting in significant population shifts.

Finally, during this period increases in population were occurring in the outlying areas encompassing West Roxbury, Hyde Park, and Roslindale, which also received the major portion of the city's new single-family and multifamily construction. Most resembling the suburbs in terms of housing types and natural surroundings, these areas attracted families who otherwise might have left the city.

The above changes are introducing important new housing demand groups. As a result of these significant population movements, long-time resident families and elderly persons, many of them with moderate or low incomes, have often seen themselves as holding the fort against new, encroaching pressures.

One such situation, best exemplified in Allston-Brighton, occurs when students and young working persons, by pooling resources and sharing apartments, bid up rents beyond the reach of local residents. Ownership turnover places an increasing share of the stock into the hands of speculators who can outbid potential owner-occupants. While demand in these areas is strong and market values are rising, the effects of absentee-ownership and inadequate maintenance are readily visible in the wear and tear of the stock. The fear of this same phenomenon is now organizing families in areas of Dorchester and South Boston which will receive the impact of the new University of Massachusetts campus at Columbia Point. (Similar speculation prevails in areas in which the expansion of major institutions is expected, as in Mission Hill, where major medical facilities are concentrated.)

Another type of situation occurs in areas where a rapid and large-scale movement of nonwhite households in search of better housing opportunities impacts on white, low- and moderate-income areas. Where this is happening—most recently in sections of Dorchester and Mattapan-Franklin—the rapid flight of the resident population (as well as of mortgage capital) is causing sharp changes. First FHA fully-insured mortgages enabled an influx of lower income households who were less able to afford housing and who had less experience in maintenance and management, resulting in decreasing property values, bank foreclosures, and accelerating abandonment. Now FHA mortgages have largely stopped and a particularly damaging type of absentee owner appears drawn to these areas—one who is attracted by the low gross rent multipliers (property values only around three times annual gross rent) and the realization that the city tax foreclosure process takes up to five years. It appears these owners do not intend to pay taxes but to pocket what rents they can while leaving the city disinvested structures to foreclose upon. Able to thus raise "their own" capital, they may have become the only buyers in these red-lined areas.

A different example of new market pressures is taking place in several reviving neighborhoods—notably the South End and Charlestown, and anticipated in the North End—where attractive location, the historical character of the housing stock, and supportive renewal activities are bringing middle-income demand into conflict with existing low- and moderate-income settlements. While general housing conditions in these areas are mixed (especially in the South End), demand is strong and investor confidence now is alarmingly high.

Thus, the housing situation in Boston's neighborhoods must be viewed as a dynamic situation in which new and old residents with varying abilities to demand housing services interact with the suppliers of housing who have varying incentives to provide such services. Also entering into this equation are the institutions which determine housing policy, either formally—like the city, state, and federal governments—or informally, like local private lending institutions. Together these factors influence the condition of the housing stock, as well as the health of the market, measured in terms of changing values, rents, and vacancies.

Index

About the Author

Rolf Goetze has been involved in the design and evaluation of housing programs in Boston since 1968. He also teaches at Boston University. His prior experiences uniquely qualify him for developing and discussing new alternatives in housing. After receiving a Master's in Architecture from Harvard in 1962, he and his wife joined the Peace Corps in Nepal, learning how people with limited resources can be aided to help themselves. Upon return to the States he worked with John F.C. Turner examining United Nations housing programs, helped found Network, Inc. and collaborated in writing *Freedom to Build; Dweller Control of Housing*, which draws lessons from both domestic and overseas housing efforts. In 1970 he completed his Ph D at MIT in Housing and Social Policy analysis, evaluating domestic rehabilitation programs. He now lives in Belmont, Massachusetts, with his wife and four children, two of whom are adopted to make "a little United Nations."